Survival Guide for Coaching Youth Softball

 **Robert B. Benson**
Tammy Benson

Human Kinetics

Library of Congress Cataloging-in-Publication Data

Benson, Robert B., 1967-
  Survival guide for coaching youth softball / Robert B. Benson, Tammy Benson.
    p. cm.
  ISBN-13: 978-0-7360-7883-2 (sort cover)
  ISBN-10: 0-7360-7883-5 (soft cover)
  1. Softball for children--Coaching. 2. Youth league softball--Coaching. I. Benson, Tammy, 1973- II. Title.
  GV881.4.C6B46 2009
  796.357'8--dc22

                                2009025547

ISBN-10: 0-7360-7883-5 (print)   ISBN-10: 0-7360-8629-3 (Adobe PDF)
ISBN-13: 978-0-7360-7883-2 (print)   ISBN-13: 978-0-7360-8629-5 (Adobe PDF)

Acquisitions Editor: Justin Klug; **Developmental Editor:** Heather Healy; **Assistant Editor:** Carla Zych; **Copyeditor:** Patrick Connolly; **Graphic Designer:** Nancy Rasmus; **Graphic Artist:** Tara Welsch; **Cover Designer:** Keith Blomberg; **Photographer (interior):** Neil Bernstein; **Visual Production Assistant:** Joyce Brumfield; **Photo Production Manager:** Jason Allen; **Art Manager:** Kelly Hendren; **Associate Art Manager:** Alan L. Wilborn; **Illustrator:** Tim Brummett; **Printer:** Versa Press

We thank Tri-Cities Girls Fastpitch Softball Association in Richland, Washington, for assistance in providing the location for the photo shoot for this book.

Human Kinetics books are available at special discounts for bulk purchase. Special editions or book excerpts can also be created to specification. For details, contact the Special Sales Manager at Human Kinetics.

Printed in the United States of America   10 9 8 7 6 5 4 3 2 1

The paper in this book is certified under a sustainable forestry program.

Human Kinetics
Web site: www.HumanKinetics.com

United States: Human Kinetics
P.O. Box 5076
Champaign, IL 61825-5076
800-747-4457
e-mail: humank@hkusa.com

Canada: Human Kinetics
475 Devonshire Road Unit 100
Windsor, ON N8Y 2L5
800-465-7301 (in Canada only)
e-mail: info@hkcanada.com

Europe: Human Kinetics
107 Bradford Road
Stanningley
Leeds LS28 6AT, United Kingdom
+44 (0) 113 255 5665
e-mail: hk@hkeurope.com

Australia: Human Kinetics
57A Price Avenue
Lower Mitcham, South Australia 5062
08 8372 0999
e-mail: info@hkaustralia.com

New Zealand: Human Kinetics
Division of Sports Distributors NZ Ltd.
P.O. Box 300 226 Albany
North Shore City
Auckland
0064 9 448 1207
e-mail: info@humankinetics.co.nz

E4665

To our three daughters—Emily, Gabrielle, and McKenna—we dedicate this book with all our love. Without your patience, support, and willingness to be our "test subjects" for new drills and ideas, we would not be where we are today. Thank you for your unconditional love.

We also dedicate this book to our late nephew, Daniel, who passed during the writing of this book. For us, the best part of coaching is the relationships we develop and the lives we touch; we remind our readers not to take these precious gifts for granted.

Contents

Drill Finder

Drill title	Beginner	Intermediate	Advanced	Batting	Bunting	Baserunning	Throwing	Receiving	Fielding ground balls	Fielding fly balls	Pitching	Catching	Page no.
Setup progression	✔			✔									52
Batting progression	✔			✔									53
Tee stations	✔			✔									54
Soft-toss stations		✔		✔									56
Batting simulation stations		✔		✔									58
Bunting progression	✔				✔								59
Bunting to targets			✔		✔								60
Running game	✔					✔							61
Two-line baserunning		✔				✔							62
Infield fly baserunning			✔			✔							64
Zigzag	✔							✔					80
Scarecrow rhyme	✔						✔	✔					81
Wrist snaps	✔						✔	✔					82
Figure eight		✔					✔	✔					83
Rocking fire		✔					✔	✔					84
Three step		✔					✔	✔					85
Relays			✔				✔	✔					86
Around the horn—counterclockwise			✔				✔	✔					87
Around the horn—clockwise			✔				✔	✔					88
Around the horn—star			✔				✔	✔					90

Preface

You may not have planned on being the head coach of a softball team, but here you are. It's your job to somehow organize a group of enthusiastic but inexperienced seven- and eight-year-old girls into a team. You may be wondering what you've gotten yourself into and whether it's too late to get out of it. But relax, Coach, this book provides the help you need. If you're feeling overwhelmed, underprepared, or maybe a little panicked, that's okay. Most coaches have shared your experience and lived to discover the joys of coaching youth players.

Survival Guide for Coaching Youth Softball is for anyone who has generously volunteered his or her time to work with young players. Whether you know little about the game or you have vast knowledge of it, this book has something for you. Teaching a seven-year-old to bat, pitch, and throw for the first time can be a challenge no matter what your background. This book provides the tools and knowledge you need to survive the first day of practice, to get your team up to speed, and to carry you through to the end of the season. Armed with this book, your sense of humor, and lots of patience, you can ensure that the youngsters on your team are having fun and learning something new.

Chapter 1 walks you through the basics of equipment and rules and how to start the season off right with a parent–player meeting. In chapter 2, you'll learn how to make the most of your practices and how to keep them fun for the kids. Chapters 3 through 6 tell you everything you need to know to teach the essential skills, such as batting, baserunning, throwing, fielding, pitching, and catching. Each of these skill chapters includes 10 drills that will make learning basic skills fun for your players. In each of these chapters, you will find beginner, intermediate, and advanced drills so you can choose the ones that are appropriate for your players' skill level. Chapter 7 covers specific offensive and defensive strategies for effective on-field execution, and chapter 8 provides everything you need to prepare for games and to manage them with confidence.

Survival Guide for Coaching Youth Softball can help you plan every detail of your season. You can also bring this book to the field with you and use it to find some drills just before practice. The book works with your schedule and provides you with the knowledge and support you need to turn your gaggle of girls into a real softball team. It can also help ensure that you and your players have fun along the way.

⚾ Acknowledgments

Survival Guide for Coaching Youth Softball is a product of years spent coaching our three daughters and their teammates. Experiencing the differences and the constants involved in coaching our oldest daughter's competitive 12U team and our youngest daughter's T-Ball team has provided us with valuable insight. Along the way, a number of individuals have provided their support and shared their knowledge; we thank them all for contributing, in various ways, to this book.

We thank our coaching mentor, the founding coach of the Washington Angels, Tammy Hutchison, for trusting us with the name "Washington Angels" and for encouraging and supporting us in our role as head coaches. Your words of encouragement, your wisdom, and your insight into life's true priorities have kept us on the road to success and helped us to create memories we'll cherish forever.

We thank the coaching staff, Traye Radach and Calvin Nash, and the young ladies who make up the Washington Angels 96 team for providing many wonderful learning and teaching opportunities. And we thank the young models who posed for the book for enduring the first 100-degree day of the year so that we could get the right shots.

We thank the coaching colleagues who not only supported us from the beginning, but also helped us to break down and simplify many of the skills and drills and to refine the progressions contained in *Survival Guide for Coaching Youth Softball*, including Kelly Richards, Larry Lozier, Greg Gott, Terry Storm, Pete Steiner, Mark Weber, and many others.

Thanks to the BCERT Class 08-01, who listened painfully and with attentive ears to drafts of parts of this book. Thank you for your patience and understanding during those hard five weeks.

And lastly we thank the Tri-Cities Girls Fastpitch Softball Association (TCGFSA) for their support over the years, for the equipment, and for the use of the facilities. You have helped to make dreams come true for countless players.

Key to Diagrams

X	Any player
X	Any player who starts with ball
X	Any player relocates to this position
B	Batter
B	Batter who starts with ball
R	Runner
P	Pitcher who starts with ball
CA	Catcher
SS	Shortstop
1B	First-base player
2B	Second-base player
3B	Third-base player
LF	Left fielder
CF	Center fielder
RF	Right fielder
C	Coach (or assistant coach or parent)
⊘	Softball
△	Cone
⊍	Empty bucket
⊍	Bucket of balls
⊥	Batting tee
▦	Backstop
⟶	Path of runner or fielder
- - - ⟶	Path of hit
⋯⋯⟶	Path of pitch, throw, or toss

Help!
Where Do I Start?

Maybe you walked into the local parks and recreation department intending to sign your young daughter up to play softball, but you walked out with a title: Coach. Afterward, as you sat in your car with a roster of unfamiliar names, a rule book, and a confused look on your face, you may have been wondering, *What just happened?* Or maybe you decided that you should do some volunteer work in your community, so you answered an ad in the local newspaper for volunteer youth softball coaches. However you became a coach—by choice or by coercion— you were probably thinking, *How difficult could it be? Doesn't everyone know how to play ball?*

On the first day of practice, though, your sense of calm may evaporate when you realize that one player doesn't know which hand her glove goes on and that another player doesn't know which side of the plate she should bat from! No matter what the situation looks like on the first day of practice, the team needs someone to rise above it all and implement positive learning experiences. That someone is you—the coach. As you watch your players chasing butterflies in the outfield and making sand castles in the infield, you must have confidence that you can help these girls become a team. You are responsible for helping the players develop their individual physical skills, teaching them good sporting behavior, and making sure they have fun every step of the way.

Coach's Equipment

Your league's rules and the age group of the players you are coaching will determine how much and what type of equipment you need. The first thing you should do as a coach is to see what equipment is provided by your local league. The following list identifies equipment that is usually required as well as some equipment that is nice to have.

- **Softballs.** Your league will probably give you a few balls to start out with. However, most coaches discover that they can never have too many softballs. In addition to throwing and hitting, you can use softballs as markers on the field in place of cones. The younger the players, the fewer softballs you will need. One bucket of balls (one to two dozen balls) will be enough if your players are under 8 years old. For players older than 8 years, you should have two to three buckets of balls because you may need to set up more batting stations.

   Softballs used in youth leagues are normally one of two sizes: 11 inches or 12 inches. The 11-inch softballs are for players 10 years old and under, and the 12-inch balls are for players older than 10. However, most leagues for players who are 8 years old and under will require 11-inch rubber balls, which are called spongy or softie balls. You should probably get some softie balls even if your league doesn't require them. These balls are more expensive, but the safety factor makes them well worth the cost. Softie balls are especially useful when kids are first learning to play the game. Using softie balls enables the players to build confidence in their skills before you put them out there with hard balls.

- **Wiffle balls.** Leagues normally do not provide Wiffle balls. However, these balls are relatively inexpensive, easy to transport, and well worth the purchase. Wiffle balls come in many sizes (golf ball size, baseball size, and softball size). You may want to have up to a dozen of each size. During live pitching drills, you can use the Wiffle balls at random. This helps the players improve their eye–hand coordination and makes them focus harder on the ball. Wiffle balls are also useful because they allow young players to get lots of swings without the risk of serious injury. However, keep in mind that the sting left from getting hit with a Wiffle ball on bare skin or other sensitive parts can be quite surprising and painful—and the players may find it quite humorous when it happens to the coach.

- **Bats.** In most local leagues, bats will be provided by the league. If you are coaching a team in the eight-and-under age group, the most critical factor you must consider is this: The bats must be light enough for the players to swing. Because of the size and weight differences of the players, the bats provided by the league may not be suitable for all players. If the bats provided by the league are not the appropriate size for your players, ask the league for some additional bats. You may also speak to the players' parents to see if this is an investment that they are willing to make. Generally, six bats of various sizes and weights should be enough to get your team through the season.

- **Batting tee.** Most leagues provide each team with at least one tee, but if your league has extras, see if you can get at least one more. If you need to purchase a tee, you should be able to get one at a sporting goods store or at discount stores for around $20. The more you spend, the better the equipment will be. However, kids can destroy a $20 tee as fast as they can destroy a $120 tee, so opting for a less expensive model makes sense when you are coaching the younger age groups. For older players—who can regularly hit the ball on top of the tee instead of hitting the tee—you may want to buy a more expensive tee that includes different position options (such as inside and outside).

- **Helmets.** Most leagues will provide helmets, but they may provide only a limited number of helmets for each team (e.g., six helmets per team). Helmets are required for each offensive player who is not in the dugout. This includes the batter, the player warming up in the batting circle (on-deck batter), and all base runners. So, in the worst-case scenario—or best case if your team is up to bat— you will have the bases loaded, a batter up, and a batter on deck, which means you'll have one extra helmet (if your team has a total of six helmets). You may want to let the parents know where they can purchase a helmet for their daughters. Helmets can cost as little as $20 at your local Walmart or sporting goods store. The best scenario is for each player to have her own helmet (for sizing as well as hygiene reasons). Each league has requirements on what types of helmets are authorized, so check with your league to make sure you are purchasing the correct type. Generally, if the helmet has a NOCSAE (National Operating Committee on Standards for Athletic Equipment) stamp on it, then the helmet will meet the league's requirements.

- **Rubber bases.** Most softball games are played on a field that already has bases. However, if your league does not have access to enough softball fields, you may be required to play some of your games on a universal field where no bases are provided. If that is the case, the league should provide the coach with portable throw-down bases. The availability of softball fields for your practices may be limited as well, leaving you with the option of practicing on a universal field or at a park. If you are playing in a grassy park, you will need something to designate the bases. This could be rubber bases or cardboard cutouts painted white. If the league does not provide rubber bases, you should purchase them on your own. They usually come in a set with a throw-down pitching rubber. You can find a complete set at most sporting goods stores for around $10.

- **Backstops.** You may need some backstops, or pop-up protective nets. Backstops are primarily used for hitting balls into but can also be used to pitch and throw into. Portable backstops can cost up to $100, but are well worth the price when considering most field officials discourage hitting into fences. Backstops are not essential, but they do give players a chance to practice hitting without having to chase balls all over the field.

- **Coaching supplies.** You will need a folder or planner to hold your lineup sheets, practice plans, contact information, medical releases, and notes. Dry-erase boards work great in the dugout. Many of the boards sold at sporting goods stores are two sided: One side is for the lineup, and the other side has a template of a softball diamond. This can be used to show the players where they need to be on defense. You will also need a score book to keep track of games. Any score book will work, as long as it has enough room for you to list 15 players in the batting lineup. Again, the local sporting goods store should carry these books. If possible, designate one person (someone who will attend every game) to keep the book at all of your games. This person should read the instructions in the score book to learn how to keep accurate stats.

- **First aid kit.** Most injuries on the field can be taken care of by using the acronym RICE (rest, ice, compression, and elevation). Remember that you are not a medic, only a first responder. If a player sustains an injury that cannot be taken care of with the RICE method, you *must* notify emergency medical services immediately. Because softball is played outdoors, you may not have easy access to a phone. Therefore, you should always have a mobile phone with you during practices and games.

At a minimum, you need to have three instant ice packs (the kind you break and shake) and two rolls of athletic tape and gauze in your first aid kit. If you can't find the instant ice packs (or in case you run out), keep some Ziploc bags in your kit so you can add ice to them for a makeshift ice pack. Ice packs can be used for a twisted ankle or for a bruise that results when a player gets hit with a ball. The gauze and tape can be used for those nasty sliding burns or minor cuts. You will also need some Band-Aids to cover small scrapes. Band-Aids with famous characters from kids' shows are usually a hit. Of course, once the girls know that you have cool Band-Aids in the first aid kit, you may see an increase in the number of boo-boos that need Band-Aids. Your kit should also include Wet Ones or some type of cleaning solution to remove dirt and bacteria from open sores and cuts. You'll also want a bottle of sunscreen in the kit.

- **Catching gear.** Most leagues will supply catcher's gear for the younger ages; however, this gear may be old, and some of the straps may be missing. If you must purchase catcher's gear, go down to your local sporting goods store and bring along the girl who will be playing catcher for your team. This will ensure that you get her the proper size. Catching gear consists of a set of leg protectors, a chest protector, and a mask that has a throat protector. The connecting buckles of the leg protectors connect on the outside of the leg. Knee savers, which are pads that go behind the calves of the catcher, are another recommended piece of equipment.

- **Gear bags.** You will need a duffle bag to carry the catcher's equipment and the first aid kit. You will also need a mesh bag to carry the other equipment. A bucket can be used to carry the balls; the bucket is also useful when you need something to sit on so you can catch your breath.

- **Water cooler and ice chest.** During the spring and summer, hot days and blazing sun can cause rapid dehydration. Some fields have water fountains; however, most do not. You should have a cooler filled with ice water for drinking. You will also need an ice chest that can be filled with water and ice and at least a dozen cloths. The wet cloths can be placed over the head or neck of players to cool them down. Because the cloths will be dunked back into the ice chest, make sure that each cooler is clearly marked so the cloths don't end up in the drinking water.

Kids' Equipment

In general, the kids' equipment is purchased by the parents; however, you should check to see if your local league provides any personal equipment before you tell the parents to run out and purchase new equipment. The only required piece of equipment is a softball glove. Any other items described in this section are optional, but some are nice to have for safety reasons. You will want to go over the items at your first parent–player meeting. This will prevent players from showing up for practice wearing their dads' old first-base mitts that are four sizes too big. To help keep the kids and the dugout organized, ask your players to put their names on their equipment.

- **Uniforms and practice clothes.** Game uniforms, which usually consist of matching T-shirts, are usually provided by the league. If your league does not provide uniforms, you should talk to the players' parents at your first meeting (see "Parent–Player Meeting" section near the end of this chapter) and determine what type of uniform everyone can afford. The uniform top should be tucked in at all times. "Dress for success" is more than just words. The way players present themselves has a direct impact on how well they play. Depending on the weather, shorts or sweatpants can be worn as the uniform bottoms. You will also want the players to be dressed appropriately for practices. If possible, have the players wear the same type of clothing for practices that they wear for the games— that is, T-shirts and shorts, or long-sleeved shirts and sweatpants. Players should avoid wearing tank tops or spaghetti-strap tops. This will help prevent sunburn and scrapes and cuts to the upper body when sliding.

- **Accessories.** Every player needs a visor. Not only do visors keep the sun out of players' eyes, but they can also keep the body cooler during sunny days. Players also need to keep their hair out of their face. This can be done with a visor or hair bands. Players should not wear any jewelry (earrings, bracelets, necklaces, watches, rings, or metal hair clips) during practice or games. Most rule books state that players cannot have any jewelry exposed while playing. The only exception is a medical alert bracelet. In this case, the best option is to have the player (or parent) attach the alert to a necklace. The necklace can then be tucked and secured under the shirt, minimizing the chance of the necklace getting caught on anything.

- **Cleats.** Cleats are not required for youth softball, and tennis shoes are fine for players who are younger than eight years old. However, cleats do add to the girls' ability to stop and start fast. So as the players progress in skill, you may want to recommend that they purchase cleats.

- **Softball gloves.** Softball gloves are required for all players, and the parents are usually responsible for furnishing the gloves. Gloves come in various shapes and sizes, including infielder gloves, outfielder gloves, and catcher and first-base mitts. Infielder gloves are generally smaller and will not have a big pocket for the ball. This enables the infielder to get the ball quickly from the glove to the throwing hand. Outfielder gloves have larger pockets to help ensure that the ball does not pop out when catching fly balls. Catcher and first-base mitts have large pockets and plenty of padding because these players will receive many balls that are thrown hard. Various sizes are available for each type of glove, measuring from "youth size" to 11-inch to 13-inch gloves. The smaller the hand, the smaller the glove size needs to be. For a youth player, the most important thing is that the glove fits well, meaning that the glove stays on the hand when the player points her fingers to the ground. Youth players should also have a glove that is comfortable and has a big pocket.

  If a player's older brother or sister has an old glove lying around, the player should try that glove first. Nothing is better than a comfortable broken-in glove. If players purchase a new glove, they will need to break it in. The quickest way to break in a new glove is to oil it, put a ball inside the web of the glove, and tie it closed. The glove should then be put into a pillowcase and into the dryer (along with some old tennis shoes), and the dryer should be run for an hour on the "no heat" setting.

- **Mouth guards.** Some leagues require all girls playing the infield to have a mouth guard in at all times, unless they are wearing a face mask. The mouth guards needed are the ones that youth football players wear that can be warmed in water and molded to the player's upper teeth. This type is good because the players can still communicate without fear of the mouth guard falling out. Mouth guards can be found in sporting goods stores or in the sporting goods section of discount stores. Discuss mouth guards at the parent meeting. This will give the parents time to purchase the mouth guards and properly fit them.

- **Face guards.** Face guards (also called infielder's masks) are becoming more and more popular among youth players over eight years old. Face guards offer more protection than mouth guards because they protect the eye sockets, lower jaw, and cheeks. The cost for a good face guard is around $30, and these can be found at most sporting goods stores or online. The justification for using an infielder's mask is that the bats being made now have more "pop," meaning that the ball comes off the bat at a higher speed. Young players may not have the quickness and coordination to stop a line shot at their face. If the league does not have a requirement for the use of face guards, at least have your pitcher wear one. The pitcher is standing only 30 feet (9.1 m) from the batter, so the pitcher may not have time to get into a good defensive position if the ball is put into play.

- **Sliding pads.** Generally, leagues with players under eight years old will not allow sliding because of the risk for injury. If your league does allow sliding, then sliding pads are a must. A player's skin is no match for the dirt and aggregate that usually make up the basepaths. Sliding pads attach to the leg with Velcro straps, protecting the lower leg from getting strawberries or road rash. Keep in mind that players wearing sliding pads may still get some scrapes on their legs when sliding, so your first aid kit will come in handy. Even if you don't require the kids to slide during practice, have them wear the pads when running bases in practice. This will help the players get used to wearing their sliding pads. If the team uniform includes pants, sliding pads may not be necessary; however, sliding pads will provide additional protection and will keep a player's pants from getting torn up.

- **Water bottles.** If players bring their own water bottles to practice and games, make sure that each player puts her name on her bottle. Youth players have a tendency to forget everything that is not tied to their bodies; when a player leaves her water bottle behind, you want to be able to identify its owner.

- **Bats.** Parents frequently ask, "What is the best bat for my daughter?" At the youth level, the best bat is the least expensive bat. Bats can be purchased for around $30 at sporting goods stores or discount stores. A quick and easy way to size a bat for a player is to have the player stand straight up with her hands down to her side. Set the bat upright on the ground with the knob end upward and the barrel pointed to the ground. The knob of the bat should only go up to the player's wrist (maybe an inch past, but no more). To check the weight of the bat, have the player grab the bat with her nondominant hand and hold the bat out in front of her, with the bat pointing away from the player and the palm of the player's hand facing the floor. If the player can hold the bat for 30 seconds before her hand starts to shake, the bat is the right weight. If she cannot, she needs a lighter bat. A bat that's too light is better than a bat that's too heavy. Players who use heavy bats tend to drop their hands before they swing. When this occurs, the barrel of the bat will also drop as the player is swinging the bat, causing the player to hit pop-ups or to miss the ball altogether.

Softball Diamond

A youth softball field will usually include the following markings (see figure 1.1):

- **Infield.** The infield is the dirt portion of fair territory that's enclosed by the four bases. Whether you're playing in an eight-and-under league or on the Olympic team, the bases are 60 feet (18.3 m) apart. The only exception to this rule is in leagues that use a coach pitch program, which allow bases to be a shorter distance apart.

- **Outfield.** This area is the fair territory in the grass portion of the field located outside the infield.

- **Foul lines and foul territory.** The foul lines are chalked into the dirt starting from the tip of home plate and extending out to the outfield fence. The field of play extends from home plate to the outfield fence—which can be anywhere from 150 to 200 feet (45.7 to 61.0

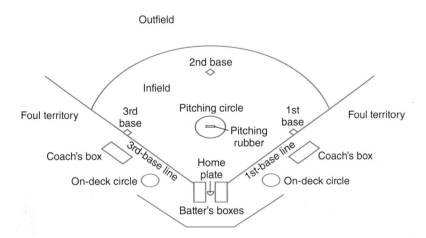

Figure 1.1   Proper markings for a regulation softball field.

m) from home plate—and between the first-base foul line and the third-base foul line. All players, with the exception of the catcher, must begin each pitch in the field of play. However, balls can be caught in foul territory to record an out.

- **Home plate, batting boxes, and catcher's box.** Batter's boxes are located on the left and right side of home plate. The catcher's box is located directly behind the batter's box. The catcher's box extends 3 feet (91.4 cm) back and runs from the outside line of one batter's box to the outside line of the other batter's box.

- **Pitching circle and rubber.** The pitcher will start out at the pitching rubber, which is located directly between home plate and second base. The pitching rubber may be anywhere from 30 to 35 feet (9.1 to 10.6 m) from home plate. The pitching circle that surrounds the rubber has a radius of 8 feet (2.4 m).

- **Coach's boxes.** Base coaches have their place as well, and that is in the boxes near first base and third base. When coaching third base, you may be tempted to run with your player all the way home and to help the umpire make the right call. However, you will need to restrain yourself if you don't want to be disqualified.

- **On-deck circles.** On-deck circles, located between each dugout and the nearest batter's box, are the designated areas in which the batter who is up next is allowed to stand to get ready to hit. This circle has a 2.5 feet (76 cm) radius.

League Rules

Generally, fastpitch softball leagues are divided into age groups that are separated by 2 years in age, such as 6U, 8U, 10U, and so on. 6U stands for 6 years old and under, meaning that the players were 6 years old on the last day of the previous year (December 31) or turned 7 the year that they registered in the 6U division. If you have a talented 6-year-old and the local league does not have a 6U division, the young player can still play on an 8U team. If you have a girl who turns 9 on January 1 of the year she wants to play, she is eligible to play in the 8U division. This is the general rule used by most sanctioning bodies; however, you should always check with your local league to verify the eligibility of all your players.

Most leagues will adopt (in part or in full) the rules of some major national sanctioning body such as the ASA (Amateur Softball Association). However, you must check with your local league for the specifics and to make sure you know the answers to the following questions. The answers provided here reflect the general guidelines that apply to most leagues and will help you get a better understanding of the game of softball.

- **What is the pitching distance and what are the pitching limits for your league?** The pitching distance may range from 30 to 35 feet (9.1 to 10.6 m) from home plate depending on the age group that you are coaching. None of the various sanctioning bodies limits how many innings a pitcher can pitch. However, most local leagues have limits for the number of innings a player may pitch per week. The reason for these limits is not so much to reduce the risk of injury as to provide equal playing time.

- **What kind of pitching is used in your league?** Most leagues start out with "coach pitch" or a pitching machine, then progress to a combination method. In the combination method, the player throws pitches until ball four is thrown to the batter. After ball four, the coach takes over and pitches to the batter until the batter hits the ball. Most leagues have a "nobody walks" rule in order to give the batter an opportunity to put a ball into play. The rule also gives the defense an opportunity to field a batted ball. Knowing the kind of pitching used in your league will enable you to determine whether you should spend any time working on pitching in practices. It will also give you a better idea of the kinds of pitches your batters will face. If your league does allow player pitching, you should be aware that it will not necessarily look like pitching. More wild balls may be thrown than strikes.

- **What are the time or run limits for a game?** Run limits per inning may be put into effect to make sure that both teams get a chance to bat. The run limits also prevent a superior team from totally embarrassing another team. At younger levels, each game may be limited to one hour in duration. Some leagues have rules that everyone bats each inning and that runs and outs do not count. If this is the case, the league may not have time limits. Sometimes the rules allow each team to get at least two at-bats, which means there will be at least two innings of play. You will need to know these details to make the correct decisions on game day, especially the decisions about how to get all the players into the game. If your league has any tournament play, the rules for these situations may be different from those in your regular games.

- **Can the players steal bases?** For players who are just starting out, most leagues do not allow stealing. But as players move up in age brackets, stealing is usually allowed. Again, knowing your league's rules on stealing will help ensure that you are not wasting limited practice time on skills that the players will not be using. If the league does allow stealing and sliding, spend time working on sliding and baserunning (see chapter 3).

- **How many players are needed to start and finish a game?** Typically, you are allowed 9 defensive players on the field at any given time. However, most leagues will allow you to play with a minimum of 8 players on the field, and some leagues may allow up to 10 players on the field. Most of your games will probably be played on weeknights, and scheduling conflicts are likely to arise for your players. Therefore, you should check your league's rules so that you are aware of the minimum (and maximum) number of players you will need.

- **Does your league use free substitution?** Free substitution is a rule that allows you to substitute players freely without jeopardy of them becoming ineligible. For a coach, this rule is great because it enables the coach to get players into play and to switch them around at will. Free substitution usually means that you can bat everybody on your team. Most youth leagues will allow free substitution, but some may have restrictions on who can substitute for whom.

- **Is bunting allowed?** In starter leagues, bunting is usually not allowed. Teaching the girls to play the game is difficult enough without adding bunting to the mix. When bunting is allowed, a youth softball game can sometimes begin to look like a game of rugby—with several players running to the bunted ball and fighting over who gets to pick it up. That being said, if your league allows bunting, you should teach your players how to bunt. Teaching this skill early helps prepare the players for higher levels of softball. At higher levels of the game, bunting (also called the short game) often becomes a critical element of the offense because it is difficult for the opponent to defend.

- **What are the pitching regulations?** The underhand pitching motion is fairly easy to learn, but it is one of the most difficult skills to master. Your specific league and the age group of the players will determine how strict the umpires will be. For most leagues, the pitcher must not take a step back to deliver a pitch, and once she steps toward the batter, one foot must remain in contact with the ground until the ball is released. When the pitcher steps on the rubber, her hands must be apart. After both feet have come in contact with the rubber, the pitcher's hands can come together only once more. (See chapter 6 for more information on proper pitching technique.)

Vital Information

Your league should provide you with a list of contact information for your players and their parents. However, you may find that this list is not all-inclusive, so you'll want to have a contact information sheet to be filled out by the parents of each of your players (see figure 1.2). Make sure you have all applicable phone numbers, including work, home, and cell phones for both parents. E-mail is probably the easiest way to communicate with

Figure 1.2   Sample Information Card for Players

Player's Information

Player name: _____ Date of birth: _____

Preferred positions: 1 _____ 2 _____ 3 _____

Uniform size: shirt _____ shorts _____ jersey # _____

(Indicate whether sizes are youth or women's.)

Parents' or Guardians' Contact Information

Main contact (parent or guardian): _____

Address: _____

Home phone: _____ Work phone: _____

Cell phone: _____ E-mail address: _____

Preferred method of contact (circle one): e-mail / home phone / cell phone

Alternative contact: _____

Address: _____

Home phone: _____ Work phone: _____

Cell phone: _____ E-mail address: _____

Preferred method of contact (circle one): e-mail / home phone / cell phone

From R. Benson and T. Benson, 2010, *Survival Guide for Coaching Youth Softball* (Champaign, IL: Human Kinetics).

your team, so obtaining e-mail addresses is essential. Before your first practice, you should determine what your primary form of communication will be (such as e-mail, phone, text, or Web posting). Your league may require parents to complete a medical information card and waivers at registration. If not, you should consider having the parents complete a form like the one shown in figure 1.3. Keep these forms with your first aid kit or in your folder so they are handy at practices and games.

Softball leagues generally require parents to provide a photo and birth certificate of their child. The league may collect these documents and send them to the sanctioning body that the league is affiliated with, but be sure to ask in case the responsibility falls to you. Additionally, your league will likely take care of insurance for playing locally. You should check with the league director and get a copy of the insurance to keep in your folder or first aid kit.

Goal Setting

Your goals for the season will vary depending on the age of your players. Make sure you have realistic expectations for the age group you are coaching, and your goals should not have anything to do with winning or losing. You need to decide what you want the players to learn in the upcoming season. You will not be able to teach every aspect of the game in one season. Prioritize what you believe is important, such as throwing correctly or swinging with the correct mechanics. Your goals may change during the season depending on how fast your players are learning.

Your players should have individual goals and the team should have goals as well. A player's individual goal might be as simple as "Not jumping out of the batter's box when the pitcher releases the ball." Other examples of goals that players can give themselves include having a positive attitude, always hustling, or running through first base every time. You should discuss player goals at the first parent–player meeting. At that time, you may want to give the players a homework assignment of writing down their goals and bringing them to the next practice.

Team goals are goals that the entire team chooses together as a group. Encourage your players to focus on their conduct and behavior rather than the win–loss record. For example, the players might focus on using good sporting behavior, encouraging each other, and hustling. Some sample goals with this focus could include "Win without gloating and lose without complaining," "High fives for every batter returning to the dugout who has just struck out," and "Running on and off the field between innings and after each at-bat."

Figure 1.3   Sample Medical Card

Player's Information

Player's name: _____

Doctor's name: _____ Doctor's phone: _____

In the event of injury or illness and your family physician is not available or is not located in the immediate vicinity and we are unable to contact a guardian, does the supervising person have your permission to seek medical attention from the nearest licensed physician or hospital?

___ Yes ___ No

If no, please specify the procedure you wish the supervising person to follow: _____

My child is covered by medical insurance: ___ Yes ___ No

Allergies, medications, and other important medical information: _____
_____

Medical Consent

Player's name _____

I, the undersigned, hereby grant _____ authority to consent to medical treatment on the above-named player's behalf should the above-named player become injured or otherwise incapacitated during any activity associated with the team.

The staff may hereby make any arrangements that are appropriate and in the best interest of the above-named player upon her injury, for the above-named player's emergency medical, surgical, or dental care. I give consent to any and all types of medical treatment or procedures, dental treatment or procedures, or surgical procedures for the above-referenced player. I give consent to the disclosure of any confidential privileged communication or information related to the rendering of any care for the above-referenced player.

A photocopy of this instrument shall be deemed an original for all purposes.

This medical consent form expires: _____
                                                                (Date)

Signature of parent or guardian: _____

Date: _____

Print name: _____

From R. Benson and T. Benson, 2010, *Survival Guide for Coaching Youth Softball* (Champaign, IL: Human Kinetics).

Parent–Player Meeting

At the beginning of the season, conduct a parent–player meeting. A successful meeting can make the difference between having a fun and exciting season and having a long and "I can't wait till this is over" type of season. The parent–player meeting is the time when you should communicate about goals, expectations, roles of all participants, schedules, and team parties. Remember, when people are lacking information, they have a tendency to assume the worst.

Before the meeting, make sure you have any information that you need to pass out. This may include rules, schedules of games and practices, directions to the playing and practice fields, contact information, blank registration and insurance information sheets to be filled out at the meeting, and sign-up sheets for items that you may need help with (such as snacks, equipment setup and teardown, and parent helpers). Make a packet for each parent that includes all of this information.

One of the first items to cover in the parent–player meeting is the role everybody has on the team and your expectations for each group of participants. Every game includes four groups of participants: players, coaches, umpires, and spectators. Players play to the best of their ability, coaches strategize and direct the players, umpires make the calls, and spectators encourage the players. Most problems that arise are the result of the participants of the game forgetting their role or trying to fulfill more than one role at a time.

Some leagues put restrictions on the teams, such as not allowing a team to meet more than three times during the week. If this is the case, and if you have two games during the week, you will be allowed to have only one practice during the week. Communicate these regulations to the parents so they'll understand your method for scheduling practices. The league will usually provide fields for your team to hold practices. Before the parent–player meeting, check with the league about field availability for the season. If the fields your league uses are heavily scheduled, be sure to make your field reservations as early as possible. It's also helpful to hold your practices every week on the same night and at the same time. This keeps things simple for you and the parents.

After the packets are passed out and while the information sheets are being filled out, you can take time to let the parents and players know what they can expect from you during the course of the season. This could include the league's rules on playing time, your philosophy of playing time, and how you plan to ensure the proper rotation of the players. Another critical item to cover is how you'd like to receive feedback from parents. At some point in the season, it's likely that a few parents may not agree with your coaching decisions. The timing of this feedback is critical. Ask the parents to wait 24 hours after the game or practice before providing any feedback. After this delay, the parents will be able to do a better job of delivering the feedback appropriately, and you'll be in a better frame of mind to receive it. Feedback should never be given in front of the players. If a parent approaches you right after a game or practice with feedback, simply remind the parent to wait 24 hours and to provide the feedback when players are not present.

The meeting is a good time to find out if any of the parents have interest or experience in coaching. You should also find out if any of the kids have experience in pitching or catching. Parents are usually more than happy to help out with practices. If they are willing to help, you should get them on board right away. Good programs don't have just one or two coaches. The best programs have many helpers sharing the load. Keeping the players busy during practices is essential because children often have the attention span of puppies. You will find it difficult—if not impossible—to run a practice by yourself. Once you have identified your parent helpers and assistant coaches, you must talk to them about your personal goals and your expectations of the players for the season.

You should also let the parents know your expectations regarding what the players will learn during the season. Some parents will want their six-year-old daughter to swing like Lisa Fernandez on the first outing. These parents may become genuinely frustrated when their daughter gets an infield base hit. You, on the other hand, may be excited when the player runs through first base after hitting the ball. Regardless of the age group, the number one priority is that your players have fun. In addition, some of the most important lessons that players will learn won't be about softball skills. Teaching players to lose without complaint and to win without gloating is just as important as teaching them the skills of the game. To ensure that everyone is on the same page from the outset, you need to communicate clear expectations regarding the behavior of the players and parents.

At the meeting, you'll also want to find a volunteer for the position of team mom. The duties of the team mom do not necessarily need to rest on one person's shoulders, nor does the person in this position have to be a mom or a woman. These duties can be split up among the parents of both sexes. However, you should designate one person to oversee all the relevant tasks. The responsibilities include scheduling after-practice snacks, team parties, and personal awards; making sure the team doesn't miss a player's birthday; and ensuring that all the parents have the team's practice and game schedule. Do not underestimate the importance of having a person in charge of arranging the snacks for after practices and games. Other than butterflies flying through the air and worms crawling in the dirt, the snacks will be the number one concern of many kids. *What are we having for snack? When do we get our snack?* and similar thoughts seem to be on the forebrain of nearly every young player.

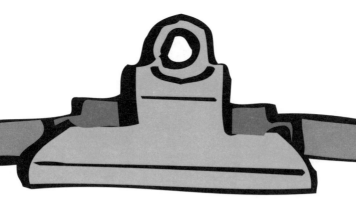

The Coach's Clipboard

✔ Check to see what equipment is provided by the league before you purchase anything.

✔ Make sure you have a first aid kit on hand for all practices and games.

✔ Understand the RICE principle (rest, ice, compression, and elevation). Use this principle when taking care of most injuries.

✔ Be familiar with the various parts of a softball diamond.

✔ Know the rules! Every league is different.

✔ Gather a contact information form for each player for easy access and reference.

✔ Gather medical information cards for each player.

✔ Set realistic goals for the team, and help your players set individual goals. When setting goals, players should focus on their conduct and behavior rather than on winning.

✔ Host a parent–player meeting early on and communicate your expectations.

✔ Designate a person for the role of team mom. The team mom will organize snacks, parties, and awards.

Organizing Your Team Practices

If you're coaching for the first time, you may fall into one of two categories: the coach who waits until the first practice is about to begin before thinking about what the team will be doing or, the coach who plans out every minute of the practice and expects the team to precisely follow the rigid schedule. Whatever your tendency, you will need a plan for making use of the practice time you've been allotted. Teaching softball skills to youngsters can be a huge challenge, and winging it just won't work. You'll have chaos on your hands. However, you'll also want to allow for some flexibility. For example, on a day when the skill instruction is getting too heavy for the players, you might decide to have a spontaneous game of tag.

Young players will develop in the right environment, and your first priority should be to provide that environment. When developing your plan, you have to "walk before you run"—and never, never, never assume anything. In youth softball, you are bound to see some players run the wrong way, or not run at all, when the ball is put into play. When this occurs at our games, we are always amazed, not at the player's reaction, but at the reaction of some of the coaches and parents, who act as if the World Series is on the line. The coach is screaming, "Run to first!" but the youngster thinks she *is* running to first and doesn't understand why her coach is yelling at her. Most likely, this coach never walked the girls around the bases during practice and told them, "When you hit the ball, run this way to first base, then turn left to second," and so on.

Shaping Your Season

Before you can start developing individual practice plans, you must first determine how many practices you will have before the first game. In most leagues, the teams will have six or more practices before their first game; in some cases, you might get fewer. Either way, you need to prioritize which skills you must teach and which skills would be good for the players to know before the first game. Again, your number one priority is for the players to have fun. Keep this in mind when you develop a practice plan. You want the players to come back for the next practice!

The practices before your first game will make up your preseason practice schedule. The preseason schedule should be divided into three phases: an introductory phase, a fundamental learning phase, and a skill development phase. For each of these phases, you should have an idea of where you would like to see your players' development at the end of the phase. The practices should build from the previous practice. You may not cover everything that you set out to do, but having goals will enable you to see if you are still on track.

The introductory phase should consist of two or three practices. This is where you introduce all the skills and establish terminology, routines, and expectations for your players. The fundamental learning phase is where the players learn all the skills they need in order to play the game. You will spend the majority of your preseason time (two to seven practices) in this phase. In this phase, you break the skills down into parts, and the players master the separate components of each skill (using the various drills provided in this book). The skill development phase should start no more than two practice sessions before your first game. This phase continues throughout the rest of the season when the games start. For these practices, you incorporate the entire defense on the field, along with base runners, so that the team can work on defensive and offensive situations. The players are put in gamelike situations, and they work on the mental aspect of the game.

During the introductory and fundamental learning phases of the preseason, you may want to divide the offensive and defensive skills into separate practices. This can help prevent your players from being overwhelmed with new information. During the fundamental learning phase, you can repeat offensive and defensive drills from one practice to the next. The players will simply perform them better and faster at the subsequent practices. When you get into the skill development phase of your practice schedule, you can practice offensive and defensive skills in the same practice. You can cut portions of the skills as needed to focus on the areas that need the most work. You can control the time by increasing or decreasing the number of repetitions done in the drills.

Assessing Skill Level

Early in the preseason, evaluate your team's level of ability in the following skills: batting, baserunning, throwing, catching, fielding, and conditioning. Defensive strategies and the responsibilities of each position will come later (in the skill development phase of your practice schedule). Knowing what to do with the ball won't help a player if she doesn't have the skill to execute the play. By assessing your players early in the season and reassessing throughout the season, you can determine how to best use your time in practices. You will be able to focus on the areas where your team needs the most help.

Designing a Practice Plan

There is nothing worse than when a young player walks up to you and asks, "What's next, Coach?" and an uncomfortable silence fills the space as you try to determine what to do next. To prevent this, make a plan for each practice that specifies what will be covered from the beginning to the end. For each practice session, you should set objectives that identify the skills (or portions of skills) that need to be worked on to make sure the team accomplishes what you want for that practice. Each objective will have a series of activities or drills that can be done to accomplish the objective. An example of one objective for the first practice would be "Getting to know your teammates and coaches." Some activities that may be used to meet this objective would be introductions and playing a name game.

Identifying objectives will help you keep things on track toward achieving success in the long run. To start out with, you may want to limit the number of objectives to no more than four per practice. However, it is better to have too many objectives than not enough. If you don't get to an objective during the practice session, you can cover it at the next practice. The key is to keep the kids moving. If you run out of things to do, it will look as if you are not organized—and when a coach appears to be unorganized, the kids will sometimes take over the practice with questions, horseplay, and all-out anarchy.

Most of your objectives for practices will come from evaluating the team's development during prior practices or games. If the players can't throw or catch the ball, then the team needs to work on that. For each objective, you need to identify up to six activities or drills that will be done in the practice session to meet the objective. To determine the activities and how much time to spend on each objective, you may use root cause analysis. For instance, say your players are having trouble hitting the ball; to identify the root cause of the poor performance, you will need to identify the part of the swing that most of the players are not performing correctly and plan activities that address this problem area.

Every practice should start with the objective of warming up the players so they are ready mentally and physically to play the game. After a brief warm-up, you'll want to have the kids do some stretching. (Chapter 8 provides detailed information about pregame warm-ups and stretching. You can use this material for your practices as well.) You should also consider adding a cool-down period and some static stretching at the end of practices. When pressed for time, you may have trouble squeezing this in, and with kids this age, it may not be essential. However, getting the players in the habit of cooling down is a good idea. At a minimum, show your players how to stretch their major muscle groups so that they can do it on their own after practice. Sometimes, something simple such as having players help you round up the equipment from the field can work as a cool-down.

Figures 2.1 and 2.2 provide sample practice plans (a defensive and an offensive plan) that would be suitable for the fundamental learning phase of the preseason. These examples incorporate building on muscle memory and using progressions (see the next section) to teach and develop a skill. As the players develop their skill level, you can also incorporate modifications and competition into the drills to make them fun.

Using Progressions

In chapters 3 through 6, the basic skills of softball are discussed in detail. As you will see, all skills can be divided into parts. By teaching a skill in parts, you will help your players learn the skill quickly and gain confidence in what they are doing. A progression refers to a set of drills that are done in sequence to reinforce muscle memory of good mechanics. Each drill in the progression covers one of the critical elements (or parts) of the skill. Breaking down the skill into parts will provide feedback for the coach and the players to help determine if more work needs to be done in that area. It will also reinforce muscle memory to help players perform the skill correctly when going full speed.

When I (Bob) first started coaching five-year-old boys and girls, I was an assistant coach helping out the head coach. We just just put the players into positions and hit or threw balls to them. We expected the players to be able to perform the skill because we had showed them how to do it. Frustrations ran high, and we sometimes forgot that we were dealing with five- to seven-year-olds, not high school athletes. Of course, the players could sense our frustration, and soon they did not want to practice anymore because they were not doing well. Skills such as batting,

Figure 2.1 Sample Defensive Practice Plan

Duration	Objective	Activities or drills
10 minutes	Warming up and improving conditioning	*Log Tag:* Players lie down in a big circle in the outfield in pairs of two; each team forms a "log." One girl is named "it" and has to run around the outside of the circle and tag another player, then run around the outside of the circle at least one complete time and get back to her log before being tagged. The player who was tagged is now "it" and must try to touch the player who tagged her before she gets back to her log; if she fails to do so, she must tag another player. *Static and dynamic stretching* *Two-Line Baserunning drill* (see page 62)
15 minutes	Practice throwing components	Throwing progression: 1. *Wrist Snaps drill* (see page 82) 2. *Figure Eight drill* (see page 83) 3. *Rocking Fire drill* (see page 84) 4. *Three Step drill* (see page 85) 5. *Relays drill* (see page 86; rotate after 3 reps) 6. *Around the Horn drills* (see pages 87, 88, and 90)
15 minutes	Practice fielding components	Fielding progression: 1. *MCPC Cadence drill* (see page 105) 2. *First-Step Quickness drill* (see page 103) 3. *Feeds drill* (see page 106)
15-20 minutes	Improving fielding	*Cross Lines drill* (see page 108) *Shortstop Hole drill* (see page 110) *Outfield feeds* (see page 114)
2 minutes	Practice baserunning and improving conditioning	*Running Game drill* (see page 61)

From R. Benson and T. Benson, 2010, *Survival Guide for Coaching Youth Softball* (Champaign, IL: Human Kinetics).

Figure 2.2   Sample Offensive Practice Plan

Duration	Objective	Activities or drills
10 minutes	Warming up and improving conditioning	*Log Tag* (see page 25): 5 minutes *Static and dynamic stretching* (dynamic stretches beginning at the foul line) *Two-Line Baserunning drill* (see page 62)
10 minutes	Practicing batting components	Loading progression: 1. *Batting Progression drill* (see page 53): 10 reps of motion-critical-pitch cadence 2. *Batting Progression drill:* 10 reps of motion-critical-pitch-yes-bang-bang cadence 3. *Batting Progression drill:* 10 reps of motion-critical-pitch-yes-bang
40 minutes	Improving batting	Batting circuits (10 minutes each then rotate): 1. *Batting Simulation Stations drill* (see page 58): use motion-critical-pitch-yes-bang-bang cadence 2. *Soft-Toss Stations drill* (see page 56) 3. *Tee Stations drill* (see page 54): use full swing 4. *Live pitching* (front toss) by the coach (see page 57)
2 minutes	Practice baserunning and improving conditioning	*Running Game drill* (see page 61)

From R. Benson and T. Benson, 2010, *Survival Guide for Coaching Youth Softball* (Champaign, IL: Human Kinetics).

throwing, and fielding are complex skills that professional athletes have trouble perfecting, and most professional athletes break down the skill into separate components to become better. When teaching a new skill to an undeveloped player, breaking the skill down to make it easier to learn just makes sense.

We use progressions to teach the three main skills of softball: batting, throwing and, fielding. These progressions are discussed in the skill chapters (chapters 3 through 5). Any of the drills in this book can be used individually, but using a progression is often the most efficient and effective method for teaching young players new skills.

Surviving the First Practice

The first practice of the season will be more of an introductory practice than a formal offensive or defensive practice. For this practice, a good strategy for the coach is to follow the rule of three: Give three bits of information and then do a fun activity. For example, you can start by introducing the girls to each other. Then introduce the coaches. Next, go over the expectations for how players are to conduct themselves during practice. And then do a fun activity. If you have a lot of new players, a good activity is to see who can remember everybody's name. Give a reward to anybody who can. Of course, it's likely that no one will be able to do this the first time around, so everyone will need to introduce themselves again.

You could then bring the players back into a circle and talk about what the team practices will look like. Explain to the players that the number one goal for the season is to have fun and learn softball. Then explain that the best way to do this is by having an excellent attitude, being responsible, hustling, being prompt—and at all times, respecting teammates, coaches, opponents, parents, and umpires. By this time the players will be bouncing in their seats again. To help them burn off some energy, you may want to pick a tree in the distance and have a foot race to it and back. When the players return, have them grab their gloves or bats or both.

Your first practice may not have any drills whatsoever, and that is okay. You're better off spending this time playing "follow the leader" by walking the players around the bases. While doing so, show the players what direction to run, and name the bases as you go. Again, this is an introductory practice. You are introducing the kids to the game, to each other, and to you, the coach.

However, this is a good time to introduce some of the concepts. It's true, Coach, some of your players may not know the most basic softball terms. Take time (use the rule of three) to introduce the girls to the concept of being on offense and what kinds of equipment they'll be using when they're on offense. You can show them what a tee looks like and why they would use it. Also show them how to put a helmet on. Of course, this is a good time to check the fit of the helmets for each girl. Start emphasizing the importance of safety in preparation for upcoming batting practices (see chapter 3). Then give them a fun activity to do and have them move with their gloves to the pitching circle.

Now you can introduce the defense. Have the players put their gloves on. Explain why catching a ball with fingers up is safer than with fingers pointed down (refer to chapter 5 for more details). Describe what a good athletic position looks like. Do another fun activity, and then walk the baseline and introduce the bases and what to do on each base. While walking around the bases, you can stop at each defensive position and explain the position. Describe what defensive players will look like when fielding the ball at each position and what they will do with the ball if it is hit to them. You should also explain the trip around the bases from an offensive perspective—that is, explain that circling the bases and touching home plate means that the offensive player has scored a run. Again, don't take anything for granted, especially with beginners.

You can use a game to introduce the defensive positions in the outfield. Have the players start at home plate and race to one of the three outfield positions and then back to home. The coach calls out the outfield position that they should run to (i.e., left field, center field, or right field). This burns energy and helps the players learn where each position is located. For this game, use three parent helpers (or you can use players) to go stand in those positions before you start.

Making Practice Fun

Many kids are not born with competitive blood running through them, but they do enjoy having fun! Unfortunately, many coaches focus on teaching young players how to be competitive, and soon the game is no longer fun. Competitiveness is a result of confidence that is built through a series of successes. Including drills in your practice that incorporate skill development is the most effective way to keep the players coming back and wanting more. Before you know it, the players will be challenging themselves to push themselves harder, and they will be developing skills without knowing it.

Part of making sure everyone has fun is to make sure that every player is included in each drill or game at practice. Teaching young players that every position on the team is important will prevent anyone from feeling left out. This can be a challenge in youth softball, especially when it comes to the outfield positions. Frankly, not many balls get hit out there. Most kids want to be in the middle of the action. This is one reason for adopting the philosophy that every throw needs to be backed up—in both practices and games (see chapter 7). Strategies such as this can help ensure that your outfielders participate even if all the action is in the infield. You can also emphasize that communication needs to take place with every throw by every player on the team.

Another way to keep practices fun is to incorporate a fun drill or activity at the beginning, middle, and end of every practice. A fun idea is to bring water balloons to practice. You can just throw them around, or you can use them in some of the drills described in this book. Throwing Frisbees is also a fun way to get the girls to run after a flying object. If you are not having fun, then the players will not have fun either. Remember that the real work of the practice can be fun too. You can incorporate competitions into drills and let the players come up with the consequences for the losing team. The players get to use their imaginations, and when you laugh, it gives them permission to laugh as well.

Assigning Player Positions

In youth softball, as in any youth sport, it is difficult to predict which players will develop in size and speed as they grow. Therefore, you should give all players the opportunity to play in every position on the field during practice and games. We have been coaching one group of players for five years (since the time they started in the 8U recreation division). No one would have guessed that the shortest girl on our team would be the best first-base player, but that turned out to be the case. She continued being our first-base player until we needed to fill another key position, catcher. She is still one of the shortest players on our team, and she can still play first base as well as the biggest player on the team. You will have players like her who don't "fit the mold," but as long as they can play the positions with confidence, they will do fine, especially at an early age. The following are some guidelines regarding what types of players are most effective at each position; however, we remind you that these are only guidelines.

- **Pitchers.** A good defensive team always starts on the mound. Many of your players will hound you relentlessly to let them pitch. In youth softball, every player should be given the opportunity to pitch. The key to being a good pitcher is not just the player's size, but also her drive to learn and her ability to stay committed. You are looking for players who can whip the ball rather than aim the ball across the plate. Accuracy comes with muscle memory, but it is difficult to try to teach a player to snap the ball at the release point.

- **Catchers.** The catcher is arguably the second most important position in softball. Again, you will not have a shortage of players who want to put the gear on. Because of all the neat gear, youngsters often think that catcher is the "coolest" position—that is, until the player has to catch during a game. Being the catcher is a ton of work. A good practice is to rotate players out every inning or two. As the players get older, they may be able to handle a complete game.

- **First base.** Besides the pitcher and catcher, the first-base position is the most important position on the field. If you don't have a pitcher who can strike batters out, you may want to put your most athletic player at first base. This is a great defensive strategy. Of course, a tall left-hander would be ideal for first base, but height is not the most important thing. You need a player who is not afraid to dig the ball out of the dirt and is aggressive going after balls not thrown directly to her (which will be many balls).

- **Middle fielders.** The shortstop and second-base positions are considered the middle fielders. Players in these positions need to be quick laterally and must be able to cover a large area.
- **Third base.** Third base is considered one of the corners. (First base is the other corner.) Typically, taller players who have quick reflexes are best suited for third base. (These are often players who have not yet developed their foot speed.)
- **Outfielders.** Players who can catch a fly ball usually get the nod for the outfield. The center fielder needs to have the quickest reaction off the ball; this player must cover ground rapidly. The center fielder also needs to be the most vocal because she is in charge of the outfield. In youth softball, the outfielders usually do not get a lot of action. For this reason, you can play the outfielders right on the edge of the grass. In this position, they'll have a better chance of having a ball hit to them. When players start hitting the ball farther, you can move the outfielders back.

Rotating the players through all the defensive positions is a good strategy early in the season. However, it can be confusing for the players because each position has different responsibilities. As the players progress in their skill set, find out where they like to play and where they are good at playing. At a minimum, each player should have the opportunity to learn one infield position and one outfield position.

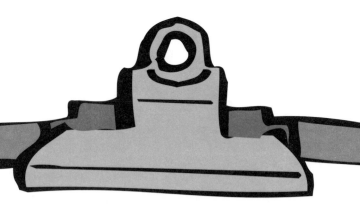

The Coach's Clipboard

✔ Put together a plan before your first practice.

✔ The preseason practice schedule should be divided into three phases: introductory phase, fundamental learning phase, and skill development phase.

✔ The skill development phase should not start until two practices before your first game and should continue throughout the season.

✔ For each practice, you should have a goal, objectives (a list of skills to work on), and activities that will be used to accomplish the objectives.

✔ When teaching skills, you should break down each skill into parts to help your players learn the skill quickly and gain confidence.

✔ Your number one goal for your first practice is to survive it. The next goal is to make the practice fun so your players will return for the next practice.

✔ As a coach, your main goals for your players are that they have fun and that they get better after each practice.

✔ Rotate players so that the players get a good understanding of each position. This will also give you the opportunity to see who performs best at each position.

Teaching Offensive Skills With 10 Simple Drills

In softball, the offensive skills consist of hitting the ball, running 60 feet, and turning left. Running and turning are fairly simple, but hitting a pitched ball is one of the toughest assignments you can give a youngster. You may see your players randomly swinging the bat long before or after the ball passes them by. Others may never want to take the bat off their shoulders. If your players behave like this, don't be discouraged. You're not alone.

This chapter covers the basics of batting and running the bases, including what players should do when they get on base. It's never a good thing when you have two base runners occupying the same base, but you are likely to see this occur more than once. When you begin teaching basic skills, you will need to start from the very beginning. For example, in a batting practice, you may be tempted to rush right into drills, only to discover that many players don't know how to hold the bat properly.

A good rule to follow as a coach is to not expect anything from your players until they fully understand what you expect of them. To make your expectations clear, you must take time at the beginning of the season to front-load the players with information about basic skills by giving them numerous demonstrations and explanations. As players begin to grasp the skills, you can cut back on (or entirely eliminate) the demonstrations and explanations. You can then focus on making sure the girls get lots of repetitions as they practice the skills.

Batting

Whether your league uses a batting tee, coach pitch, a pitching machine, or live pitching, you should teach the same approach and setup for batting. Young players must first learn the proper way to stand in the batter's box and the proper way to hold the bat. In the first batting practice, walk the girls over to the two batter's boxes. Explain that the batter's box a player will use depends on whether she bats left or right handed. When you are standing at home plate and looking toward the pitcher's mound, the box on the left side is for righties, and the box on the right is for lefties.

Because hitting the ball is one of the most difficult things to do in softball, you should introduce batting as early as you can. Have the players do some type of batting drills on the second or third day of practice and during every subsequent practice. At a minimum, every other practice should include some batting drills.

The younger the players, the more strict a routine you should teach them to use as they enter the batter's box. As the players get older, they will develop their own style. Some will smack home plate a set number of times or twirl their bat clockwise a set number of times. Until they find a routine that works best for them, you will have to provide one for them. Don't worry about being accused of "cookie-cutter" coaching, because the players will take ownership of what they do at the plate sooner than you may want them to.

Bat Safety

When you begin teaching young players to bat for the first time, your practice can quickly turn into chaos. If you're lucky, you will escape practice without getting whacked by an inadvertent swing. Be warned, this is where a good thing can go bad!

To ensure everyone's safety, explain to the players how you expect them to handle a bat. Be sure to do this *before* you pass out the bats. The primary rule is that when any player has a bat in hand, the barrel of the bat should be pointed down. When moving from station to station in practice, players should drag the barrel on the ground. Bats should only be swung when a player is at a designated batting station with adult supervision. To ensure the safety of your players, you must enforce these rules. If a player swings her bat around inappropriately, have her take a time-out; if the behavior continues, have her sit out of batting drills for the day.

For all batters, the basic routine consists of five steps: approach and setup, stance, load, swing, and finish. At each batting practice, give the players time to do the same routine when stepping into the box before every practice swing. Many variables come into play whenever a player steps to the plate in a game, including wild pitches, runners on base, and sometimes even hand signals from the coach. If the player's batting routine is automatic, the player will have one less thing to worry about as she tries to focus in on the next pitch. And don't forget to have the players practice running to first base after they hit the ball. Come game time, this will save you from having to yell "Run, run, run!" every time a player hits the ball.

Approach and Setup

For the approach and setup in the batter's box, teach your players to stop just outside of the box before getting in. The process described here would be just the opposite for a left-handed batter. The batter should first step her right foot into the box, and then her left foot. She should plant the left foot just at the front of the plate; her feet should be slightly wider than shoulder-width apart. After positioning her feet, the batter should hold her right hand up to the umpire and ask for "time." The request for a time-out gives the batter about 5 to 10 seconds to get ready before the pitcher is allowed to pitch the ball. The umpire is not required to give the batter time to get adjusted; however, umpires will usually honor the request and hold their hand up to indicate that the pitcher should wait. Once the time-out is given by the umpire, the batter will then adjust her distance from the plate. When the batter is situated, the umpire may point to the pitcher and will say something to the effect of "play ball."

The batter can properly adjust her distance from the plate by holding the bat with one hand (the left hand if she is batting right handed) and extending her arm and bat so that the tip of the bat touches the opposite side of the plate. She may need to bend slightly at the waist to reach. If she bends too far and starts to lose her balance, she is too far from the plate. The batter must be able to hit a pitch that is thrown to the outside of the strike zone without losing balance or lunging. When a player finds a comfortable distance, the player should position herself in the same way every time she goes up to the plate. The position will vary from one batter to the next.

Stance

The stance is the position a batter assumes when resting in the box and getting ready for the pitcher to start her motion. The feet should be shoulder-width apart with the toes facing forward. The bat should rest

Figure 3.1 Proper stance for resting in the batter's box.

Figure 3.2 Proper alignment and position of the hands for gripping the bat.

on the throwing shoulder, which should be the shoulder closest to the catcher (see figure 3.1). The bat should be at a 45-degree angle to the ground, and the player's head should be turned slightly toward the pitcher; both eyes are looking at the pitcher.

To help your players learn the proper way to grip the bat, teach them to remember three landmarks. The first landmark is that the knocking (or middle) knuckles of both hands should be aligned with each other when the hands grip the bat (see figure 3.2). The weak hand (nonthrowing hand) should be next to the knob of the bat. The strong hand (throwing hand) should be up the handle toward the barrel. The hands should touch each other, and the knocking knuckles should face directly away from the batter. The second landmark is that the knob of the bat should be held at armpit level about 6 to 8 inches (15.2 to 20.3 cm) away from the body, which requires the bat to be at the proper 45-degree angle. The third landmark is that (together) the forearms should make an upside-down V shape.

For an effective and inexpensive visual aid that is fun for the players, you can create eyeball tattoos. These can be created using a marker and some white athletic tape. Place an "eyeball" on both knees and the belly button of each player. An eyeball should also be placed on the bottom of the knob of each player's bat. During the stance, the eyeballs on the knees and belly button should be looking at home plate. The eyeball on the knob of the bat should be facing the ground just behind home plate toward the catcher. During drills, you can use the eyeball tattoos to help players maintain a good position during the setup or swing. Throughout the drills, ask the players to always "check their eyeballs."

Load

The most critical step in the swing is the load. When the eyeball technique is used, the eyeballs should look at home plate during the entire loading phase. Once in her stance, the batter will need to load her hands by shifting her weight to her back leg and then back to her front leg. As her weight is shifting to the front leg, her hands start to separate from her body by moving back toward the catcher. This separation generates the most whipping force going forward. For the most efficient and effective swing, the hands need to load last and go forward last. So be sure your batters keep their hands near the rear shoulder until they start to shift their weight forward.

However, remember that you are dealing with 5- to 10-year-olds. When first learning to bat, young players will inevitably start both their load and their swing with their hands. For this reason, you should teach the players a batting progression that provides a cadence for them to follow. This is one of the most effective ways to get the batters in the right position at the right time so they swing the bat quickly and effectively. The cadence identifies critical points of the load and swing.

The *motion-critical-pitch* (MCP) cadence describes the pitcher's movements. Batters can use this cadence to get in rhythm with the pitcher and ensure that they load their swing properly. As the pitcher starts her *motion,* the batter assumes a good athletic position by bending at the knees and lifting the bat off the shoulders slightly (see figure 3.3*a*). As the pitcher starts striding forward toward the batter and commits to the pitch (which is the *critical* phase), the batter shifts her weight to the back leg and commits to the load (figure 3.3*b*). Just before or as the pitcher releases the ball (the *pitch* portion of the cadence), the batter lifts her front foot off the ground and shifts her weight forward, allowing her hands to load or separate from their starting position and move backward toward the catcher (figure 3.3*c*). After the batter's weight shifts forward, her front

Figure 3.3 As the pitcher begins her motion, the batter should assume *(a)* a good athletic position with knees bent and bat slightly off the shoulders. When the pitcher strides forward, the batter *(b)* shifts her weight to the back leg. Just before or at the pitch, the batter *(c)* shifts her weight forward and loads her hands.

toe comes in contact with the ground (this is known as the toe touch). By using the cadence, the batter will be in a good loaded and balanced position at toe touch. When batters are in the beginning stages of learning the swing, you can implement pauses to help ensure the correct body position and posture throughout the swing. Once the players have "burned in" the correct mechanics of the swing, they should then work on being fluid and smooth. Refer to table 3.1 for a summary of how the batter and pitcher move during each phase of the cadence.

Table 3.1   Pitcher and Batter Movement for the MCP Cadence

Cadence phase	Pitcher movement	Batter movement
Motion	• Starts the motion	• Assumes a balanced athletic position • Lifts the bat slightly off the shoulder as the knees bend • Relaxes and centers the weight
Critical	• Starts the stride forward • Pushes forward toward the batter, committing to the pitch	• Shifts the weight to the rear leg • Keeps the hands in the same position
Pitch	• Lands on the front foot and is releasing the ball	• Lifts the front foot off the ground • Shifts the weight forward • Lands on the front toe in a good balanced position • Loads the hands by moving them back toward the catcher just to the rear of the rear shoulder

Tee Training

Tee work is probably the most overlooked and underused training aid in softball today. Many coaches do not take advantage of the tee to help players work on correct muscle memory for the swing phase. Others do not use the tee correctly. Many players view tee work as boring and don't think it will help them hit a pitched ball. But how can players be expected to hit a moving ball squarely if they are unable to hit a stationary ball? Tee work can give your players much-needed practice.

Keep in mind that you will need to fix or replace the ball holder part of the tee two or three times during a season. Most young players cannot hit the ball squarely on a tee. Players will sometimes miss the ball completely, and they will likely hit the ball holder the majority of the time.

Swing

A good way to teach young players the swing is to explain what the lower body and the upper body (or hand path) do during the swing. The *yes-bang-bang* cadence is a useful tool for teaching the swing. This cadence is a down-and-dirty analysis of the swing phase from beginning to end and is based on the analysis of swings of elite softball and baseball hitters.

Again, once the players have burned in the correct mechanics of the swing, there will be no stopping in the motion. The batter's motion will start with the motion of the pitcher and will not stop until the swing is complete. But for the purposes of teaching the swing, have the players stop at each command of the cadence to ensure that they are in the correct position. Arguably, the swing starts during the load; however, for players learning the mechanics of the swing phase, the cadence should start once the batter has successfully loaded or gotten to the "pitch" step of the MCP cadence.

The swing starts when the front heel drops to the ground. This movement corresponds with the *yes* command of the cadence and means "Yes, I will swing at this pitch." The next command (*bang*) represents the motion of the lower body firing forward, specifically the back knee and rear elbow; the "eyeball" of the back knee will look to the pitcher (see figure 3.4*a*). The second *bang* command represents the motion of the hands firing forward (figure 3.4*b*), and now the "eyeball" on the belly button and on the knob of the bat will look to the pitcher. As mentioned earlier, the hands will fire forward last! Table 3.2 provides a summary of how the body should move during each phase of the cadence.

Figure 3.4 As the batter completes the swing, she *(a)* fires with the lower body, and *(b)* fires with the upper body.

Table 3.2   Batter Movement for the Yes-Bang-Bang Cadence

Cadence phase	Lower body	Upper body
Yes	• Front heel goes down as weight starts shifting forward. • Front leg needs to be firming up as the weight is being transferred from rear leg and as swing progresses.	• Hands and upper body do not move yet.
Bang	• Rear knee drives forward, lifting the back heel straight up to start the hips turning toward the pitcher.	• Hands and upper body do not move yet.
Bang	• Front leg accepts all the weight and starts firming up to prevent the upper body from moving forward during the swing.	• Belly and bat knob turn toward pitcher. • At contact, rear elbow drops toward hip, and front elbow leads the hands as if throwing a Frisbee. • Hands move directly toward the pitcher (rear hand is palm up; front hand is palm down). • Both arms extend straight out toward the pitcher, making a triangle with arms and shoulders. • Rear shoulder should be slightly lower than the front shoulder at contact and through extension.

When the batter's hands fire forward, they should continue forward until the arms are at complete extension with both arms facing out toward the pitcher (see figure 3.5). This keeps the barrel of the bat on plane with the ball path longer, increasing the hitter's chances of hitting the ball. At extension, the rear shoulder should be slightly lower than the front shoulder, and both shoulders should be turned so the player's chest faces the pitcher. The uneven shoulder position allows the batter to keep her eyes on the ball, get her frame behind the bat, and get her arms to extension. If the shoulders remain completely level during the swing, none of these elements can happen. The hand position should remain the same through the swing and to extension. The palm of the front hand should face down and the palm of the back hand faces up. The hands should roll over only after the arms reach full extension.

You will probably be amazed at how many parents are hitting coaches. Some common advice you will hear parents giving their young player is "Lift your back elbow." And it is true that all elite hitters flare their rear elbow as their hands separate from their body. However, the elite hitters don't need to be told to lift their back elbow; the elbow flares automatically if they load their hands correctly during the load. When the rear elbow is farther from the body, the batter will get more separation, but this will also make it more difficult to hit the ball. We tell our young players to keep the rear elbow near the body as they load their hands.

Figure 3.5 Proper extension for the swing.

That being said, all of the power hitters on the 12U competitive team flare their back elbows to one degree or another, but they haven't been told to do this. If you teach the fundamentals of the swing, the power will come when the players get confidence that they can hit the ball. If necessary, you can share the breakdown of the hitting basics with parents to help them understand your methods.

Finish

The batter's shoulders finish the rotation as the bat wraps around the body; the hands should finish near the front shoulder now with the bottom hand facing up and the top hand facing down. With the batter still in a balanced position, the weight now starts to transfer back to the rear leg. All the "eyeballs" (the front of the knees, the belly button, and the bottom of the bat knob) are now looking at the pitcher.

Bunting

For safety reasons and to keep the game basic for beginners, very few leagues allow bunting at the beginning youth level. Bunts can be dangerous. To bunt effectively, the batter turns and faces the pitcher, exposing her front side and hands to any wild pitch. In general, bunts are used by more competitive teams to keep the defense off guard and to force the defenders to make plays they are not used to making. Of course, for young players, most plays are plays they are not used to making, so the offense doesn't need to bunt to catch the defense off guard. Furthermore, in leagues for young players, most of the hits resemble a well-placed bunt anyway. This is called the swinging bunt, which is practically impossible to defend.

The need to teach your young players how to bunt depends on whether or not the league allows bunting and how much time is allowed for practices. However, you may consider using bunting drills even with the youngest of players. Bunting drills help young players build confidence quickly, and bunting forces the batters to focus on the ball making contact with the bat. If your league does allow bunting or if you want to use bunting drills, you will need to teach your players the two types of bunts: the sacrifice bunt and the bunt for a hit. The sacrifice bunt is used to advance runners from one base to the next. With this type of bunt, there is no secret about what the batter is going to do; the batter shows bunt early and tries to place the ball 5 to 10 feet (1.5 to 3.0 m) in front of the plate. With this bunt, the batter is often called out at first base. The bunt for a hit is more difficult to defend. The batter looks as if she is trying to hit the ball for a home run, but at the last second, the batter bunts the ball, taking the defense by surprise.

For sacrifice bunting, the setup for a bunt consists of two elements: a position in the front of the batter's box so the batter is as close as possible to the pitcher and a grip that places the batter's hands up the handle of the bat close to the barrel. Moving up in the box improves the chance of bunting the ball into fair territory because the front of the box extends in front of home plate and into fair territory. Moving the grip closer to the base of the bat's barrel gives the batter more control of the bat head so she can more easily make contact with the ball.

The load for the sacrifice bunt consists of turning completely to the pitcher so the batter's knees and belly button are facing the pitcher. The batter will have a slight bend of the back knee and will have the rear elbow "connected" to the hip or side of the ribs. The barrel of the bat should be at the top of the strike zone and at an approximate 45-degree angle.

The batter should get her hands in the correct position as the pitcher starts her motion. Two methods can be used to control the bat head effectively. One is by keeping the bottom hand at the knob of the bat and moving the top hand to the start of the barrel (see figure 3.6a). The other is by moving the bottom hand to the middle of the bat and the top hand one half of the way up the barrel (see figure 3.6b). Either way is fine, but the batter's hands should separate to give the player more control of the

Figure 3.6   Proper technique and hand positions for bunting.

bat. Players should try both methods and should use whichever method gives them more control over the bat head.

The only thing left to do is make contact with the ball. Contact should be made out in front of the body toward the pitcher; this keeps the ball in fair territory, and the batter has better vision out in front. If the ball is pitched low, the batter should bend her knees and maintain the same bat angle while she makes contact—the barrel of the bat should be higher than the hands.

Bunting for a hit, unlike sacrifice bunting, is intended to catch the defense off guard so the batter does not show that she is bunting until after the pitcher has released the ball. This way the defense thinks the batter will swing at the pitch and they will stay back in their normal defensive positions, meaning they have further to run to get the bunted ball. With a bunt for a hit, the batter usually makes it to first base safely.

Baserunning

Baserunning is often overlooked in practices, but it can be the most discouraging part of a game to watch. Few players under eight years old will flat-out run when running the bases. You can work in practice to help them improve in this area, but be prepared to see players running loops around the infielders, tripping over bases, or not going to the base at all because it is being heavily guarded by four girls of the opposing team—none of whom has the ball.

Early on, the key principle you want to teach base runners is simply to *run to* and *through* each base. Most young players tend to slow down five feet or so short of each base. They do this for one of three reasons. First, they are afraid of being hit by a badly thrown ball. Second, they believe the throw will beat them, so they give up. Third, their equipment does not fit them properly. If a young player's helmet is too big, her helmet may fall down over her eyes when she runs hard, causing her to slow down to adjust it so she can see where she is going.

To fix the first problem, teach the base runners to run aggressively to every base and to turn their head away from where the throw is coming from. Also teach them to slide (except at first), if your league allows sliding, when it looks as if a play is going to be made. To fix the second problem, teach the base runners that they should never give up because defensive players often make throwing and catching errors. At the youth level, a base runner always has a pretty good chance of making it safely to the base. The equipment problem is easy to fix: Get a helmet that is the correct size.

Base Runners at Bat

The batter becomes a base runner as soon as she puts the ball into play. Each batter will need to know how to react to the different ways the ball can be put into play: ground balls hit to the infield, ground balls or line drives hit to the outfield, and fly balls hit to the infield or outfield.

Ground Ball Hit to the Infield
On a ground ball hit to the infield, the batter should get out of the batter's box as quickly as possible without taking any more steps than needed. After swinging, the batter should bring the back foot forward toward first base and run in a straight line toward the base. When running, the player should focus on the spot beyond first base where the dirt from the infield meets the grass from the outfield. This is usually about 10 to 15 feet (3.0 to 4.5 m) beyond first base. For proper running form, the player needs to place her weight on the balls of her feet like a sprinter, not overstriding and not chopping. The player's hands should be moving from her cheeks to her hips and the elbows should be bent in a 90-degree angle. The player should keep her elbows close to her body, pumping her arms to make her run faster.

Players should step on the front outside corner of first base (figure 3.7), looking down and to the right as they pass through the base. Looking down and to the right will help runners avoid being hit in the face by badly thrown balls. It will also allow them to see if the ball was overthrown. Tell the players to watch their foot touch the base. This will keep the runner leaning forward with her head down as she reaches the base, which may prevent her from slowing down. Players should run through first base by at least two steps and then use short choppy steps to slow down, lowering their body by bending their knees. They should turn to the right, or to the outside, to return to the base. This will give them another opportunity to see if the ball was overthrown. In addition, turning out enables them to return to first base without risk of being tagged out. If a runner turns in toward the infield (i.e., toward second base) after crossing first base, the umpire and other players might assume that the runner is trying to advance to second base. In this situation, the runner can be tagged out even if she is just returning to first base.

Figure 3.7 Proper technique for stepping on first base for a ground ball hit to the infield.

Ground Ball Hit to the Outfield

Many youth leagues only allow one base per hit, which speeds up the game and prevents the continuous game of fetch that can occur when fielders overthrow a ball to a base player. This rule also prevents a batter who bunts from getting an infield home run as a result of errors by the defense. If your league uses this rule, you can still have your players prepare to advance to second base when they hit the ball to the outfield, even if they can't actually take second base.

If the batter hits the ball to the outfield, she will need to get out of the box the same way as when she hits a ground ball to the infield. But on an outfield hit, the runner needs to head in a straight line toward the first-base coach's box instead of first base. When the runner reaches a point a little more than halfway up the first-base coaching box, she will make a hard angle toward the front inside corner of first base (see figure 3.8). The runner should step with her right foot against the front inside corner of first base as she makes the turn toward second base. To help players maintain balance while making the turn, tell them to lean into the turn to

Figure 3.8 Proper technique for stepping on a base when rounding the bases.

the point where they would fall over if they weren't moving so fast. Remind them to accelerate through the base on every turn!

Once the runner has cleared first base, she will need to locate the ball immediately. At this point, the player should listen to the instructions from the first-base coach; however, your players also need to know how to handle the situation on their own. Occasionally, first-base coaches get caught up in admiring a hit, and they forget that they have a runner to coach. If the rules allow, encourage your players to keep running if they believe they can make it to the next base without being thrown out. Even if a runner gets thrown out when advancing to another base, you should praise her for her aggressiveness. These sorts of actions may cost the game, but they can provide a far better reward—that is, helping the players develop confidence and teaching them to play aggressively and to take chances.

Fly Ball Hit to the Infield or Outfield

Of the many frustrations you may face as a coach, none may drive you closer to the edge of insanity than when the following scenario occurs: Your batter hits a pop-up with a hang time of about 20 seconds to the shortstop, the shortstop drops the ball, and yet the batter is still thrown out at first base. Instead of running to the base, the batter was walking back to the dugout, kicking the dirt and getting ready to throw her helmet because she was certain that the ball would be caught.

Depending on the age group, your players may take from four to six seconds to reach first base after hitting the ball. Therefore, if things went correctly in the previous scenario, the batter would be on second base looking to go to third before the shortstop even had a chance to miss the ball. In the interest of your own mental health, teach your players to run down the baseline as soon as the ball is hit! In fact, you can sweeten the deal by explaining that on fly balls the batter usually doesn't have to worry about beating the throw to first base because she can be on base before a fielder has a chance to make a play on the ball. Teach your runners to sprint hard on all pop-ups and to try to end up on second base before the ball is caught. The fielders will usually not be expecting the runner to be heading to second base. Consequently, if a fielder drops the pop-up, the fielder will not be prepared to throw out the runner.

Base Runners on a Base

Once a batter gets on base and the play is over, that batter becomes a base runner. For any given at-bat, your team may have a base runner already on first, second, or third base (or any combination of those bases) when the ball is put into play. The responsibilities of these runners are similar to when they were trying to get on base, though a few differences are worth noting, including base-to-base situations and how to lead off from a base. Although your players need to know the basics of these skills, be aware that these skills are learned through experience and that most players will not master these skills until they have a very good understanding of the game.

Leads   The ASA and NSA rules both state that players cannot leave the base before the pitcher releases the ball. Some leagues, though, do not allow runners to leave a base until the ball is hit. Before you hold a baserunning practice, be sure you know the specific rules of your league. Two methods of leading off a base can be used. In both methods, players should place their left foot on the base. The first is the traditional style in which a player places the right foot forward off the base and keeps the left foot on the base (see figure 3.9). The second method is the rocker style in which the player places her left foot on the base and places her right foot off and behind the base (see figure 3.10). If your league requires players to stay on base until the hit, the traditional leadoff gives runners a stride advantage over the rocker style. If your league allows runners to leave the base after the pitch, then the rocker-style leadoff—if timed right—can be a split second faster because the player is in motion toward the next base before leaving the base.

Regardless of your league's rules, nothing will happen before the pitcher delivers the ball, so you can use the MCP cadence (described

Figure 3.9 Proper position for the traditional leadoff.

Figure 3.10 Proper position for the rocker-style leadoff.

earlier in this chapter) to help your players learn to leave the base efficiently. Use the following guidelines for each leadoff method:

- **Traditional leadoff.** During the motion and critical part of the cadence, the runner should get her body in motion by leaning back. Then, she should try to time leaving the base with the motion of the pitcher's release (pitch) of the ball. The runner should try to be in motion and ready to explode when the pitcher's arm is at the top of the circle. Tell your players to keep their shoulders and hips squared to the next base; they should then push off the base with their rear foot and drive their head and shoulders forward to explode into the leadoff.

- **Rocker-style leadoff.** As the pitcher rocks back and begins her movement (motion), the runner should rock back, shifting weight to her rear leg, and the runner's arms and hands should go up over her head. The shoulder and hips should be squared up to the base she is running to. As the pitcher strides forward and as her arm reaches the top of the circle (critical), the runner rocks forward, shifting weight to her front leg and bringing both of her arms back down and past her hips. As the arms pass the hips, the player strides forward with the rear foot toward the next base, leaving the lead foot still on the base. Shortly after the stride foot of the pitcher lands and as the pitch is being released (pitch), the runner's left foot should be coming off the base and taking her second stride toward the next base.

Buckets, Cones, and Bodies

Only three situations call for a player to run directly down the basepath to the next base. The first is when the player hits a ground ball to the infield and needs to get to the base quickly and or run through first base. The second is when she is trying to steal the next base. The third is when she is at third base and runs home. To run for extra bases, players must learn to use a path other than the basepath. Players need to know how to take the proper angles as they round the bases. Buckets, cones, and bodies can be used to give visuals to the players on where they need to run. Use cones to specify the inside part of the angle that players should take around first base, then position the buckets to identify the outside part (the area that runners need to stay inside of as they approach first base and make the turn). If you don't have any buckets on hand, you can use bodies. Have a parent volunteer or an assistant coach stand just past first base so your runners can't round into right field.

For both leadoffs, teach your players to explode off the base every time. This prevents the defense from knowing whether the player is going to steal or just lead off and read the play. The push-off should happen just before or as the pitcher releases the ball (if this is allowed in your league). Runners should keep their shoulders and hips squared to the forward base, and they should drive their head and shoulders forward to explode into the leadoff. For the first two or three steps, the player should tuck her chin into her chest and should be looking at the ground a few feet in front of her, as she would be in a full-out sprint to the next base.

If the player is just leading off (not stealing), she will need to lift her head up and look at the batter to see if the ball is being put into play. The runner will start to slow down and turn toward the batter to read the play: Did the batter hit the ball? If so, is it a ground ball, a pop fly, or a foul ball? Did the pitcher throw a wild pitch? Did the ball get past the catcher (passed ball)? The runner must quickly determine the situation. As a general rule, the leadoff for runners on first and third base should be a body length plus a stride. At second base, the leadoff should be a body length and two strides. This is because the pickoff throw from the catcher is shorter to first and third base than it is to second base. The lead at third should be more conservative because the runner is now in scoring position—and frankly, it's hard work for a team to get a player to third base, so you don't want them to mess up at that point. Regardless of which base a player is on, the following tips can help runners make good decisions on base:

- In general, a runner should not be in a hurry to get back to the base on leadoffs. She should watch the pitcher catch the ball from the catcher. The runner should make sure the pitcher is in the pitching circle *before* moving back to the base.

- The runner should look for ways to get to the next base. Good opportunities to advance to the next base occur when the catcher makes a bad throw or when the pitcher drops the ball.

- The runner should always keep her eye on the ball until she has made a decision to advance to the next base or return to the base she just came from. When the player makes a decision to go to a base, she must commit to the decision and run hard!

- If the catcher pops up with the ball, the runner should take one hard step back toward the base. The runner should keep her eyes on the ball and the catcher.

- If the catcher pops up and throws, the runner should take a hard crossover step back and then find the base quickly.

- If a runner needs to dive back to the base, she should reach out with straight arms and with fists clenched to prevent injuries to her fingers. She should land on her thighs and belly, not on her hands and knees. To prevent injuries to the face and throat, she should turn her head away from where the throw is coming from.

Base-to-Base Situations

In youth softball, the number one rule for baserunning is that trail runners do not pass any other runners in front of them. Chuckle if you will, but it's more common than you might think. You will undoubtedly see this occur at least once during the upcoming season. In a recent game we coached, a 7-year-old player on an 8U team got passed in the area between second and third base. She was on second base talking to the center fielder (a summer friend) about who knows what. Neither the runner on second nor the center fielder noticed when the ball was hit sharply to right field. When the runner from first base got within five feet of the runner on second, she started yelling at her to *run!* The runner on second then remembered that she was playing softball, and she started running. But the runner from first passed her by.

Getting your young players to focus for every pitch while they are standing on a base might seem next to impossible. If you are able to find players who can accomplish this task and who do not make baserunning errors, then you should jump for joy! However, your players are more likely to behave just like all the other 5- to 10-year-olds in the world. Because five seconds is about as long as you can expect a young player to focus at any given time, you should ask your players to give you five seconds of focus on the start of every pitch. During this five seconds of focus, the base runner needs to be aware of how many outs there are, and she must know what she will do when the ball is hit. The following tips can help your base runners know what to do when the ball is put into play:

- **With fewer than two outs.** For ground balls, the players must run aggressively to the next base, making sure they do not interfere with the defense trying to make the play. For high fly balls, the base runners should tag up (see page 148 in chapter 7). For line drives, the base runners should freeze and watch the ball hit the ground before advancing to the next base.

- **With two outs.** In this situation, the base runners should run on everything, including fly balls, ground balls, and line drives. The only exception would be when they do not have a runner behind them and there is no force play at the next base.

Scoring is fun, and when players get the hang of running hard and aggressively, they will be running for fun. Your players also need to learn how to avoid running into an out when they run hard and aggressively. Running into an out occurs when a runner runs right to a defender who has the ball. This can happen when a runner is going from first to second and the ball is hit to the second-base defender or when a runner is going from second to third and the ball is hit to the shortstop. The defender does not have to do much work to pick the ball up and tag the runner as she runs past. The general rule for avoiding this situation is that if the ball is hit and fielded in front of a runner, the runner needs to stop and watch the defender make the throw before advancing to the next base.

When a base runner has made it to second or third base, she is now in scoring position. A hit to the outfield should advance any base runners from second or third base to home. With that in mind, the batter should run hard and aggressively to second base, anticipating that the defense will try to get the runners who are trying to score. And lastly, when runners are on second and third base, the runner on second can take a bigger lead because the defense will be more concerned about the runner on third (the lead runner). If the defense throws to the base of any runner other than the lead runner, the lead runner can break for home and try to score.

Drill 1 Setup Progression

EQUIPMENT   Athletic tape; a marker; a bat for every player

PURPOSE   This drill teaches players the proper setup and stance for batting.

PROCEDURE   Children love games and tattoos, and this drill uses both. Tear off lots of two-inch (5 cm) strips of athletic tape and draw an eyeball on each strip to create tattoos. Place an eyeball tattoo on each player's knees and on her shirt at belly button level. Also put a tattoo on the bottom of the knob of the player's bat. Arrange the players into a large circle around you in the infield, spacing them out far enough so they won't hit each other when they swing a bat. If you have a dirt infield, you can stand on the pitching mound, and each girl can draw a batter's box and home plate in the dirt (cardboard cutouts of home plate work well too). Each player should face you as if she is expecting a pitch from you at any time. Start with the players outside of the box. When you say "Stance," the players step into the batter's box using the proper routine. When you say "Motion," the players respond by getting into a good athletic position while keeping their eyeball tattoos looking in the proper direction. Do 10 to 12 repetitions of this setup routine.

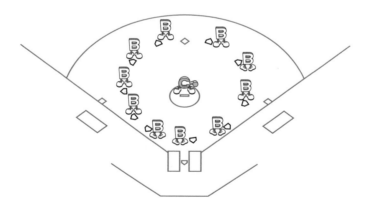

COACHING POINTS   During *stance,* all the eyeball tattoos on a player's body should be looking toward home plate. The eyeball on the bat should be looking down toward the ground just behind the plate toward the catcher (if one were behind the plate). This position ensures the proper bat angle of 45 degrees. During the repetitions, walk around the circle and watch each girl do at least one rep.

Drill 2 Batting Progression

◎ BEGINNER

EQUIPMENT   Athletic tape; a marker; a bat for every player

PURPOSE   This drill teaches players the proper load and swing.

PROCEDURE   As described in drill 1, place eyeball tattoos on each player's knees and shirt and on the knob of the bat (see photo). Arrange the players into a large circle around you in the infield, spacing them out far enough so they won't hit each other when they swing a bat. Each player should face you as if she is expecting a pitch from you at any time. You will call out the cadence "motion, critical, pitch, yes, bang, bang." For the first 12 reps, you should pause for one or two seconds at each command. These reps are considered a static phase in which the players assume the key positions with deliberate precision. Have the players hold each position for one or two seconds so they will be able to feel the technique and start to develop the proper muscle memory.

COACHING POINTS   The best time to use this drill is right after running the Setup Progression drill, while the players are still in the circle. Make sure you "check the eyeballs"—during the load, the direction the eyeball tattoos are looking (toward home plate) should not change. At the completion of the swing, all the eyeball tattoos (knees, belly button, and bottom of bat) should be facing the pitcher (the center of the circle).

MODIFICATIONS   At the beginning of the season, you may want to start this drill with 12 reps that just include the load (motion, critical, pitch) and then add on the swing (yes, bang, bang) for another 12 reps. When the players have mastered the full cadence, you can work on timing by simulating the motion of the pitcher while the batters call out the cadence. Make sure they say "Pitch" before or as you release the ball; otherwise, the batters will be late with their swing. You can eventually move on to calling out one "bang." On that command, the batter combines the final two steps into one fluid motion.

   You can also incorporate live pitching into this drill. From the center of the circle, pitch Wiffle balls to a batter who calls the cadence. The rest of the batters do dry swings. Work your way around the circle so each batter gets a pitch.

Drill 3 Tee Stations

EQUIPMENT   Batting tee, bucket of softballs (or Wiffle balls), bat, and backstop (or space on a fence or the backstop behind home plate) for each station. If a backstop is not available, players can hit into an open field.

PURPOSE   This drill teaches players the proper swing mechanics.

PROCEDURE   For each station, set up a batting tee in front of a backstop. At each station, a player will set up to hit the ball into the backstop, and a coach (or parent) will be there to supervise. The number of tee stations you set up depends on how many batting tees, backstops, and coaches are available. The remaining players will form equal lines at each station. The coach places a ball on the tee. The batter completes 5 batting reps with the coach calling out the full batting cadence (motion-critical-pitch-yes-bang-bang). The batter pauses at each command and does not proceed until the next command is given. After the last *bang* command, the batter swings the bat and hits the ball off the tee. For the next 5 reps, the coach only calls out one *bang.* On that command, the batter combines the lower and upper body movements into one fluid motion. Then, the coach calls out 5 reps of *motion-critical-pitch-yes,* and the batter combines the movements for the *yes* and the two *bangs* into a fluid motion. Finally, the coach calls out 10 reps of *motion-critical-pitch,* and the batter combines the last three commands with the *pitch* command into one fluid motion. The batter goes to the back of the line and the next player in line takes a turn.

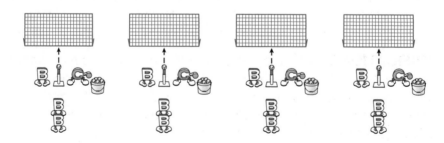

COACHING POINTS   The design of batting tees can promote bad mechanics because the location of the ball holder in the middle of the plate suggests that a player should make contact with the ball directly over the plate. This would be correct only if a batter sets up toward the back of the batter's box behind the plate. Be sure to have your players position themselves so that their front foot is in line with the ball holder to make sure they contact the ball at the proper point in the swing. Another critical element of tee work is that players must load correctly prior to each swing. Players may be tempted to skip this part because the ball is stationary on the tee. When performing tee work be sure to check your players' set up and swing mechanics, so they don't practice poor technique.

MODIFICATIONS   You can focus on the movement of the front or rear arm by having batters swing with just that arm. The batter's other arm should be folded across her chest with the hand touching the shoulder.

If the batters need to work on transferring weight from the rear leg to the front leg, you can have them step into the box during the reps. The batters set up outside the batter's box just as they would inside the box. They step into the box with their rear leg first, then their front leg, and then they swing the bat. The batters should not stop moving once they take their first step.

Drill 4 Soft-Toss Stations

⚾⚾INTERMEDIATE

EQUIPMENT   Bucket of softballs (or Wiffle balls), an empty bucket (optional), a bat, and a backstop (or space on a fence or the backstop behind home plate) for each station. If a backstop is not available, players can hit into an open field.

PURPOSE   This drill teaches players the proper swing.

PROCEDURE   For each station, set up a batter in front of a backstop, and position a coach (or parent) off to the side and in front of the batter so the coach can toss balls to an area in front of the batter. The coach can sit on the bottom of an empty bucket (or kneel on one knee if buckets are not available). The number of stations you set up will depend on the number of backstops and coaches you have available. The remaining players form equal lines at each station. The coach shows the ball to the batter by holding it in an outstretched hand, making sure the batter is in a good stance. The coach then lifts the ball up and says, "Motion." Next, the coach lets the ball drop down to below the waist and says, "Critical." The coach then brings the ball forward to toss it, and just before releasing the ball, the coach says, "Pitch." The coach should toss the ball consistently to a designated spot (inside high, inside low, down the middle, high and outside, or low and outside) depending on what the batters need to work on. On the outside placements, coaches must be aware that the ball may be hit right back at them if they put it too deep into the zone! After completing 10 reps, the batter goes to the back of the line, and the next player in line takes a turn.

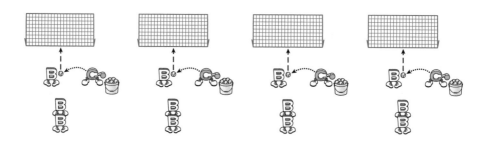

COACHING POINTS   If you are using regular softballs, you should also use a backstop if possible. If you do not have a backstop or a pop-up net, you can do soft tosses at home plate and have players shagging balls in the outfield. The flatter you toss the ball, the more it simulates a fastball. You can put more arc on the ball to simulate a changeup or a slower pitch. Soft toss is a skill to be mastered in and of itself. The better you are at it, the more beneficial it will be for the players. Because the coach says the motion-critical-pitch cadence out loud while moving the ball, the batter will be able to set up and load as she would when facing a live pitcher. Make sure that the batter is getting into the correct positions when the coach is calling out the commands.

MODIFICATIONS   You can also incorporate a front toss with this drill to better simulate live pitching. For this variation, the coach should be 10 to 15 feet (3.0 to 4.5 m) in front of the batter, and a protective net should be set up in front of the coach to protect him or her from line drives up the middle.

Drill 5 Batting Simulation Stations

⚾⚾ INTERMEDIATE

EQUIPMENT   Softballs and backstop for each station

PURPOSE   This drill reinforces a good hand path and proper joint alignment for the swing.

PROCEDURE   Position a player at each station with the backstop in front of her. The remaining players form equal lines at each station. Instead of swinging a bat, the player simulates a swing while holding a ball in one of her hands. She throws the ball into the backstop with whichever arm is holding the ball as she swings her arms and gets to extension. The coach calls out the cadence of *motion-critical-pitch,* and the player goes through the setup and load and then throws the ball into the backstop at the command of *pitch.* Have the player complete 5 to 10 throws with the front arm and 5 to 10 throws with the rear arm. The player goes to the back of the line, and the next player takes a turn.

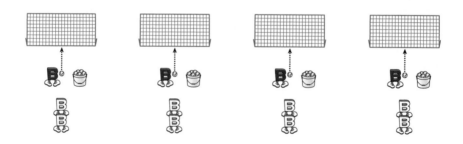

COACHING POINTS   On the throws with the front arm, watch for the following things to make sure the player has the correct hand path. If using eyeball tattoos, make sure the eyeballs attached to the knees and belly button are in the correct position during the setup and load and when the player finishes her swing. For throws with the rear arm, the throw should resemble a sidearm throw with the ball following the rear elbow, as if the player was trying to skip a rock across the water. The path of the rear elbow should be close to the side and midsection of the body.

MODIFICATIONS   If players are struggling with the motion, you can slow it down and do the entire cadence (motion-critical-pitch-yes-bang-bang) with the players pausing at each command. Make sure that the player's legs fire on the first *bang* and that the rear elbow gets "connected" with the rear hip as the rear knee fires forward. The hands should stay back until the second *bang* command is given.

Drill 6 Bunting Progression

EQUIPMENT   Balls, bats, and batting helmets

PURPOSE   This drill teaches players how to bunt correctly.

PROCEDURE   The players are arranged in a large circle, and the coach is positioned at the center of the circle. Each player is facing the coach as if she is expecting a pitch from the coach. The players should have eyeball tattoos (described earlier) on both knees and on their belly button. The coach calls out the cadence of *motion-critical-bunt,* and the players assume the correct positions at each command. The players' initial stance and their response to the *motion* command look exactly the same as for the batting progression. At the *critical* command, the batters should separate their hands and get a bunting grip on the bat. At the *bunt* command, the batters square

around toward the pitcher so that all three eyeball tattoos are looking at the pitcher; the batter should be bending at the knees (see photo). The coach gives the cadence for 12 repetitions.

COACHING POINTS   On each command, have the batters hold the position, and check their eyeballs. Also check to make sure that the bat is at the top of the strike zone. The only movement of the bat should be down.

MODIFICATIONS   Do a second set of 12 repetitions in which the coach simulates the motion of the pitcher while calling out the cadence. Then progress to having the players call out the cadence as the coach simulates the pitching motion. Eventually, you will want to progress to actually pitching balls to the players. When you start pitching balls from the center of the circle, give one pitch to a batter and then move to the next batter, making sure the rest of the players say the cadence. The player who is actually bunting should be focusing on bunting and should not say the cadence.

Drill 7 Bunting to Targets

⚾⚾⚾ ADVANCED

EQUIPMENT   Bat, batting helmet, bucket of balls, and six cones

PURPOSE   This drill teaches placing bunts in specific locations.

PROCEDURE   Set up three zones on the infield by placing three cones down the first- and third-base lines 5 feet (152 cm) apart. The first cone is 5 feet from home plate. Draw an arc-shaped line in the dirt connecting the cones on each baseline (from the first cone on the third-base line to the first cone on the first-base line, and so on). Draw another line in the dirt from home plate to the pitching mound; this line will split the arcs in half. The coach is positioned approximately half the distance to the pitcher's mound from home plate. The other players line up behind home plate. The coach pitches nine front tosses to each bunter. The batter should try to bunt each ball into the two zones furthest from home plate. (The catcher can easily pick up balls in the zone closest to home plate, and fielders can easily play a ball hit past the last two zones.) The batter tries to bunt the first three pitches to the first-base half, the next three to the third-base half, and the last three to the pitcher.

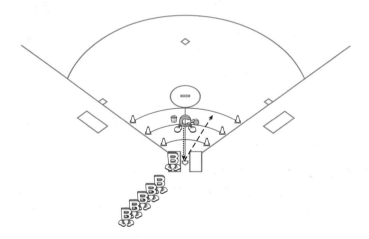

COACHING POINTS   The most common errors made by batters when bunting is that they try to push the ball to a target, which usually results in the ball being hit too hard or a foul ball. Tell your players to try to catch or absorb the ball with the barrel of the bat. The ball needs to drop out of the air.

MODIFICATIONS   To keep things interesting and competitive, score the bunts: 1 point for a bunt that comes to rest in the first zone, 2 points for the second zone, and 5 points for the third zone. Of course, all balls need to be bunted into fair territory.

Drill 8 Running Game

EQUIPMENT Bases

PURPOSE This drill improves conditioning and teaches players how to correctly run the bases.

PROCEDURE Separate the players into two equal teams. One team lines up behind second base, and the other lines up behind home plate. The teams will run a relay race around the bases. On the coach's command, the first player from each line begins running (counterclockwise) around the bases. When a player makes it back to her starting position, the next player in her team's line takes off for a lap. This continues until each player on each team has run a lap around the bases.

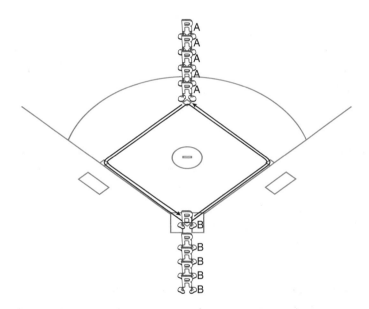

COACHING POINTS This drill is a great conditioning drill for the end of practice because the girls love it. You can set up buckets and cones to show the players the correct running path for rounding bases, or you can just have them figure it out on their own. Watch to make sure the runners are hitting the bases correctly, leaning into the base correctly, and running with proper form.

Drill 9 Two-Line Baserunning

EQUIPMENT   Two softballs

PURPOSE   This drill teaches correct baserunning and how to time a lead with the pitch.

PROCEDURE   Form two equal lines behind home plate facing first base. The two lines should be about two strides apart. One coach is positioned on the pitcher's mound. Another coach should set up at home plate to catch pitches. The coach on the mound pitches a ball to the coach at home plate. The first player in each line runs to first base when the pitch is caught. The player from the inside line runs hard to second base (figure a). The player from the outside line runs through first base and then returns to set up on the base. On the second pitch, the next player from each line repeats the same running pattern. The original runner from the inside line, who is now on second base, runs home on the second pitch (figure b). The base runner on first runs to third, touching second base on the way by. After two pitches, the bases are loaded. For every pitch thereafter, the base runner on first runs to third, and the base runners at second and third run home. When runners arrive at home plate, they go to the back of the other line.

COACHING POINTS   This drill is a great warm-up drill for the start of practices. Make sure the players running two bases take the correct angles as they are running past the first base. Watch to ensure that the girls running to first base work on not slowing down before they hit first base. Every runner on base should work on her timing of the pitcher. Before the next pitch, make sure that all the runners are ready on the bases.

MODIFICATIONS   The first two times through, have the players run flat out (no leads and reads). When all the players have gone through each line at least once, you can start working on leads and reads. The coach who is catching now allows pitched balls to get past him or her (passed balls or dropped third strike). This coach may also quickly throw the pitched balls to simulate ground balls or line drives. Runners now have to get a good lead, and they must read the ball before making a decision to advance to the next base.

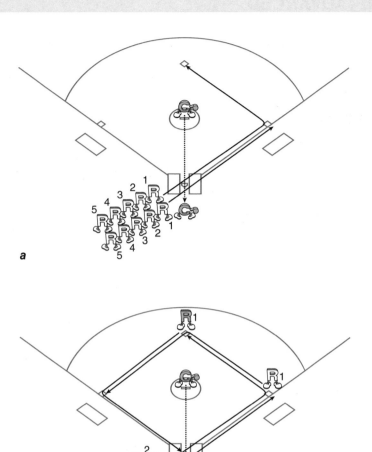

a

b

Drill 10 Infield Fly Baserunning

EQUIPMENT   Helmet and sliding pads for each runner; bucket of balls

PURPOSE   This drill teaches players how to advance to an extra base on a fly ball.

PROCEDURE   Position a defensive player at second and third base. The defensive player at second should be standing on the base. The other players line up behind home plate with helmets on. The coach, who is positioned at home plate, throws a fly ball to the player at third base. When the coach releases the ball, the first runner sprints out of the batting box, rounds first, and runs to second base as quickly as possible. Instruct the player at third base to let the ball drop directly in front of her; she should then pick it up and throw it to the defensive player at second base. The player at second attempts to tag the runner before she gets to the base. Repeat so that each player runs from home to second five times. After each time you work completely through the rotation, switch out the players in the fielding positions.

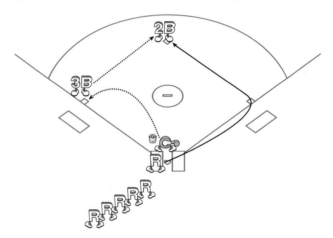

COACHING POINTS   Try to get the fly ball about 60 feet (18 m) in the air so it is similar to an actual infield fly. Watch to make sure the runner runs hard and rounds first base correctly. Chances are the runner will be safe at second. Use this to demonstrate why it's important to always run out a fly ball. In a game, the defensive player won't normally let a ball drop in front of her, but the ball could bounce off the glove or may even get away from the defensive player entirely. If the play is close at second base on the "easy" situation used in this drill, imagine what would happen in one of these realistic scenarios!

MODIFICATIONS   You can adjust this drill to simulate a situation with two outs and a base runner on second. To do this, move the line of runners to second base. Position a defensive player in one of the outfield positions and one at home plate. Throw fly balls to the player in the outfield. This player should let the ball drop and then throw it home. The runners at second base run for home as soon as the ball leaves the coach's hand.

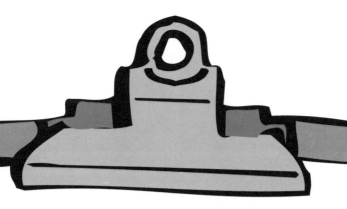

The Coach's Clipboard

✔ The number one priority for batting practices is player safety.

✔ A batter's swing consists of five parts: approach and setup, stance, load, swing, and finish.

✔ Watch for three landmarks to help ensure that a batter is in the correct setup position: Knocking knuckles are aligned, the knob of the bat is held at armpit level, and the forearms make an upside-down V.

✔ Batters can use the motion-critical-pitch cadence to get in rhythm with the pitcher's movements and to load their swing properly.

✔ The yes-bang-bang cadence is a useful tool for teaching the swing: *yes* is the front heel planting, the first *bang* is the lower body firing, and the second *bang* is the hands firing.

✔ When bunting, the batter should be up in the batter's box toward the pitcher and should move her hands up the bat handle (close to the barrel).

✔ Runners must always run hard through first base on an infield ground ball.

✔ With less than two outs, runners need to tag up on fly balls; with two outs, they should run on everything.

Teaching Receiving and Throwing Skills With 10 Simple Drills

Because nearly every play in softball includes a catch and a throw that take place under pressure (mostly coming from parents and coaches yelling with excitement), throwing and receiving are the most critical skills of the game. As a result, most games are lost by the defense rather than won by the offense. Yet, throwing is probably the most overlooked aspect of the game, leading to many errant throws and injuries.

Teaching youngsters how to properly throw and catch a ball may be the biggest challenge you face as a coach. This challenge can try the patience of even the calmest person, and it will surely accelerate the aging process for you, Coach. Teaching these skills requires many repetitions and close monitoring. In the beginning, some players won't be able to throw the ball without looking like contortionists, and you'll likely see lots of thrown balls pass right by the intended targets. This chapter explains the proper grip of the ball and proper throwing and catching mechanics that will take the players from looking as if they're swatting flies to making hard, accurate throws.

A brief word of caution is in order here, too. Never use a hard ball when teaching any new skill to young players, especially throwing and catching. Use tennis balls, sponge balls, or softie balls when players are trying these skills for the first time. Nothing can discourage and scare beginning players more than having a hard ball coming right at them. In addition, because the players' aim may not be right on target, it's much safer for everyone involved—maybe even the spectators—if the players aren't using hard balls when they first attempt throwing.

Techniques for Catching a Thrown Ball

Many coaches spend plenty of time teaching their players how to throw the ball properly but fail to teach them how to catch it properly. Most injuries in softball result from being struck by a thrown or batted ball, so you must make sure that your players know how to catch a ball. The initial reaction of many players to having a ball coming right at them may be to move out of the way. The worst approach you can take is to throw a hard ball at a young player who is struggling with her fear of being hurt. Unfortunately, many coaches and parents use this technique to try to help players overcome their fear. When using softie, sponge, or tennis balls, the players know they will not get hurt, and they can concentrate on catching and fielding the ball correctly. Then, when the players have gained confidence that they can stop a moving object, they will be able to field and catch a ball without hesitation.

When getting ready to catch a ball, a player needs to be in a good athletic position. The player should have flexion in the hips, knees, and ankles. Make sure that players receiving the ball are giving a good target with their gloves; they should have their glove out in front of them "demanding" the ball. If the player is not ready for the ball, she will not be able to react to it quickly, and she will likely miss it.

When preparing to catch a ball, the player should be moving to the ball. She should catch the ball in front of her, and her elbow should be flexed. When making the catch, the player should step forward and outside the path of the ball with her glove-side foot. The foot should be planted before the catch is made. Getting to the outside of the ball's path with the lead foot will be an easier task when the ball is moving to the glove side. However, when the ball is traveling to the throwing side, many players' feet seem to be stuck in concrete—the players just reach their glove hand across their body and hope the ball gets there. Remind the girls to step to the ball with their glove-side foot. When the ball is to their left or right, they may need to step farther with the glove-side foot to get in the proper position.

Players should catch the ball with their hands in either a fingers-up or fingers-down position depending on whether the ball is coming at them above or below the waist. If the ball is above the waist, the player must catch it with her fingers pointing up (see figure 4.1a); if the ball is below the waist, the player must catch it with her fingers pointing down (see figure 4.1*b*). Explaining the fingers-up and fingers-down position to five-year-olds can be challenging. To demonstrate this concept, have each player hold her glove hand straight up above her head; the palm is facing away from the player (to the front), and the fingers are pointing to the sky. Then, have the players make a big semicircle with their arm, moving the arm down to the side of their body and keeping the palm facing away from them. The position of the hand as it goes around the circle is the position that it should be in when catching a ball. As the hand drops below the waist, the players will be able to see that their fingers start pointing to the ground (a fingers-down position).

An effective way to help players learn to catch the ball correctly is to toss tennis balls, sponge balls, or softie balls to the players from a distance of about 5 feet (152 cm) away. Start out throwing the ball above the player's shoulders so she must catch it with her fingers up. Then throw the ball a little lower each time. As you start throwing the ball lower toward the player's waist, the player may have a tendency to back up so she can catch it with fingers down (like catching it in a basket) above the waist. This is a common mistake that young players make when catching a ball. When a player uses a fingers-down position to catch a ball above the waist, the ball will often come out of the glove, popping up and back. And when this occurs, the next thing in the line of the ball is the player's chin or face. This is another reason you do not want to start out using hard balls.

Figure 4.1 When catching a ball *(a)* above the waist, the hand should be in a fingers-up position; when catching a ball *(b)* below the waist, the hand should be in a fingers-down position.

Throwing Grip and Release

Before you begin teaching the mechanics of throwing, you'll need to cover the proper grip on the ball. Good news, Coach, the grip is the easy portion of the skill to teach. You may have heard of two-seam and four-seam pitches or throws. These terms relate to how many seams cut through the air as a ball rotates. How the player grips the ball determines whether the ball will have two seams or four seams cutting through the air after release. When a ball is thrown correctly, it will also have backspin. The ball is spinning *true* when the spin is a straight 12 o'clock to 6 o'clock spin from the thrower's perspective (or a 6 o'clock to 12 o'clock spin from the receiver's perspective). A four-seam ball will go farther and faster than a two-seam ball. A two-seam ball or a ball that does not have "true" spin tends to drift left or right.

Now, before you try to explain the difference between a two-seam and a four-seam throw to a group of six-year-old girls, let's review the proper grips for each. For a two-seam ball, rotate the ball until the seam creates an upside-down U (or horseshoe shape) with the curve of the seam at the top of the ball. As shown in figure 4.2, the middle finger should be positioned at the top center of the upside-down U with the pad of the middle finger resting on the seam; the thumb should be placed on the opposite side of the ball from the middle finger. The other fingers should contact the ball where they rest naturally. Players with small hands may not be able to fully grip the ball with their middle finger and thumb on opposites sides. These players may need to slide their thumb toward their index finger.

For a four-seam ball, turn the ball so that the seam creates a backward C. You can simply rotate the ball a quarter turn clockwise from the upside-down U position. To throw a four-seam ball, place the middle finger at the top and center of the C, and place the thumb on the seam at the opposite side of the ball (see figure 4.3). Again, the other fingers rest in the location that's natural. Because of the size of the ball, players with small hands may have trouble getting a good grip with the middle finger and thumb on the seams on opposite sides of the ball. In this case, you may prefer to have these players use a two-seam grip.

A common visual aid can be used to keep things simple for the younger girls and to make it easier for the coach to evaluate throws. Use black tape to mark each ball with a continuous stripe over all four seams of the ball, making sure that you stay in the center of the seams. You can now instruct the players to put their middle finger on the tape where it intersects the seam and to put their thumb on the tape on the opposite side of the ball. The tape should run under their middle finger and under their thumb. In addition to helping the players learn the grip, the tape

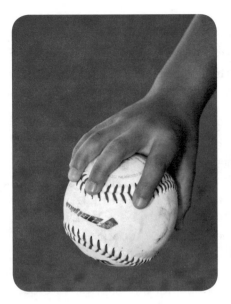 

Figure 4.2 A correct two-seam grip.   **Figure 4.3** A correct four-seam grip.

gives you immediate visual feedback when the ball is in flight. If the ball is spinning correctly, the black tape should be vertical. Any variation from the vertical line is an indication of either a bad grip on the ball or a bad release. This trick isn't merely for youngsters; take a look at any major college team's warm-up, and you will find they have a bucket of balls with tape on them.

Even when players use the correct grip, the release affects whether a throw will have a true spin on the ball. Most kids release the ball by rotating their wrist to the outside. In this position, the palm faces the inside of the body, the fingers roll to the outside of the ball, and the thumb rotates up at release. The proper release is when the wrist snaps forward and down so that the thumb is pointing down at the finish. Again, to keep things simple for the kids, tell them to pretend that they are painting with their middle fingers and that they should paint their target while releasing.

Throwing Mechanics

For your players to learn proper throwing mechanics, you must teach them to use an appropriate arm circle: The arm should start out front and sweep past the thigh on the way back, and the elbow should travel above the shoulder on the forward motion. With a circle motion, the arm does not stop during the throw; therefore, there is less strain on the shoulder. Early in the season, the players may have sore shoulders, but this should last only until their muscles get in throwing shape.

Slight differences exist between the technique for throwing from the infield and the technique for throwing from the outfield. However, young players under 10 usually lack the strength to throw the ball hard, so you may only need to teach them how to throw like an outfielder. An outfielder uses a big circle and takes a strong stride, sometimes even hopping to get as much power as she can with her legs. Having players use the big swooping arm circle of an outfield throw is also a good way to avoid injuries while helping your players develop proper mechanics.

As the players get older and faster, an infielder will not have time to wind up with a big arm circle. At that point, you can teach them the infielder throwing technique, which allows them to get the ball quickly to their throwing shoulder by not sweeping the arm past the leg. The arm circle for an infielder should be smaller and look more like an oval, and it should occur just below the shoulder. The key is that the arm does not stop or stall in the launch position. An infielder's steps are shorter and more deliberate. An infielder relies more on her arm strength and quickness to deliver the ball.

The throwing motion consists of four basic components for the upper body and three steps for the lower body. Of course, the throwing motion is really an extension or completion of catching or fielding the ball; therefore, the motion begins just after the player has caught or fielded the ball (the ball is in her glove). The basic components for the upper body are *securing* the ball with the throwing hand while the ball is in the glove, *separating* the ball from the glove and body, *snapping* the arm to the target, and *following through.* You can teach the first three parts as the three Ss. It's easy for the kids to learn "secure, separate, and snap." If these parts are done correctly, the follow-through will happen naturally. But in the beginning, you should make sure the players follow through correctly because they may not generate enough forward momentum to automatically follow through on their own.

For powerful and accurate throws, the lower body needs to move in conjunction with the upper body. Table 4.1 provides a comparison of what the upper body is doing in relationship to the lower body during the throw. The three steps for the lower body start when the glove-side foot steps toward the ball as the player is catching or fielding the ball. The timing and placement of this step are critical because the catch should happen almost immediately after the foot is planted. The placement of the step should be on the outside of the ball's path, allowing the player to catch the ball between the center of the body and the outside of the foot placement. On the second step, the throwing-side foot strides past the front foot as the throwing hand is securing the ball and separating it from the glove. For the third step, the glove-side foot steps toward the target and lands in front of the other foot in line with the target. This step should occur as the elbows are being stretched apart and the throwing

Table 4.1   Upper- and Lower-Body Movements for Throwing

Component of throw	Upper body	Lower body
Secure (Glove-side foot has already stepped to the ball, and the ball has been caught or fielded.)	• Pull the glove back to the center of the body. • Secure the ball with the throwing hand in the glove using the correct grip on the ball.	
Separate	• Separate the ball from the glove, pulling the ball down and back to start the arm circle.	• Step with the throwing-side foot past the other foot. • Plant the throwing-side foot at a 45- to 90-degree angle. • Stride toward the target with the glove foot.
Snap	• Throw with the elbow leading above the shoulder. Pull the glove toward the heart.	• Firm up the front leg. Push with the back foot.
Follow-through	• After the ball has been released, the arm should be long and loose, finishing across the body with the hand touching the opposite hip or upper thigh.	• Drag the laces of the back foot across the grass.

arm is moving in a circular motion. The forward motion of the arm happens when the foot is planted and the leg starts firming up.

Secure   Securing the ball is more than just grabbing the ball from the glove to throw it. The player needs to secure the ball quickly and with the correct grip and hand placement while setting up for a hard, accurate throw. Securing the ball should happen immediately after the catch and the first step with the glove-side foot. The player should pull the glove to the center of the body, slightly below and in front of the throwing shoulder. This allows the glove shoulder to start turning toward the target. The throwing hand should already be at the glove or meeting the glove as the glove is being pulled back. The grip may not always be a true four-seam grip; however, the important thing is that the players are *feeling* for the seams and that their middle finger and thumb are on opposite sides of the ball. Generally, it will take years for players to develop the ability to immediately grab a ball with a four-seam grip, so starting them young just makes sense.

Two methods are commonly used to bring the hands together to secure the ball in the glove. The first method is usually used by infielders and catchers who need to make quick throws. In this method, the player brings the hands together with the fingers on each hand pointing up (see figure 4.4a). The position looks as if a player is putting her hands together to pray. For the second method, which works well for the types of long throws that outfielders routinely make, the hands are more out front as if they are clapping (see figure 4.4b). The player pulls the glove to the center of the body, slightly toward the throwing side and below the throwing shoulder. The palm of the throwing hand should face up, and the palm of the glove hand should face down. This sets the player up for a good arm circle.

Figure 4.4 Securing the ball can be done with (a) the hands together and the fingers pointing up or (b) the hands in a clapping position with the palm of the glove hand down and the palm of the throwing hand up.

Separate   Separating the ball from the glove should involve a fluid motion that allows the player to get into a correct throwing position. The correct throwing position is having all the joints in the body in the line of force when the player reaches the fully separated position. The line of force—also known as the power line by pitching coaches—is the imaginary line between the thrower and the receiver. During the separation, the player takes the second step of the throw by striding past the first foot with the throwing-side foot and planting it at a 45- to 90-degree angle to the inside (see figure 4.5). Because few, if any, six-year-olds understand what a 45-degree angle is, you can simply tell them to point their toes out when taking their second step. The foot placement designates the starting point of the line of force. The ending point of the line of force is the target.

On the third step, the player steps with the glove-side foot, and that foot lands on the power line with the toe pointed toward the target (or pointing slightly inward). As the player starts the third step, she should pull the throwing arm (with the ball) down and back past the thigh of the throwing-side leg to start the arm circle. The clap style of securing the ball allows the throwing hand to pull the ball easily down and back. This style also forces the shoulders to rotate and forces the body to get into the correct throwing position as the player separates the ball from the glove. If your players are using the pray style of securing the ball, they can immediately pull the glove to the throwing shoulder, where they can separate the ball from the glove with the throwing hand. Your players need to separate their elbows to prevent them from pushing the ball, which is a common pitfall for beginners using the pray style of separation.

The fully separated position, or launch position, occurs when a player completes the third step and the ball has traveled back and away from the body to its farthest point (see figure 4.6). In this position, all the major joints should be in the line of force, including the feet, knees, hips, shoulders, and elbows. The glove side is facing the target. The hands are at the farthest point away from each other, and both hands (and the ball) are in the line of force.

Figure 4.5 To begin the separation, a player steps with the throwing-side leg and plants the foot with the toes pointing out.

Figure 4.6 On the third step, a player steps with the glove-side foot, planting the foot on the line of force, and the hands are at the farthest point away from each other.

The separation portion of the throw is the most difficult step for most young players to perform. Don't be surprised if you see a wide variety of movements and timing issues. Most young players have the tendency to push the ball rather than throw it. Helping them learn the arm circle along with the steps will cure most bad habits because the players are forced to turn their bodies sideways to the target.

Snap   An effective snap relies on the timing between stopping the forward momentum of the body (with the front leg) and decelerating the throwing elbow. With proper timing, the ball travels past the elbow and stops for a split second at a consistent release point somewhere out to the side of the body and above the head (see figure 4.7). Although the snap occurs at the arm, it actually starts with the feet. When the front foot lands on the third step, the foot should land on the line of force and should be pointed to the target (or have the toes facing slightly in). The front leg should be slightly bent, absorbing the forward momentum and then firming up as it stops the momentum. The rear leg pushes forward, causing the hips to rotate or pop to the target. All this movement in the legs happens while the throwing arm is separating from the body and reaching the farthest point back that it will travel. As the hips rotate toward the target, they cause the upper torso and shoulders to start following the rotation. Once the body has rotated back so it is facing the target, the body stops or decelerates to allow the arm to catch up and whip over the shoulder. The elbow needs to be bent between 90 and 120 degrees and needs to be at shoulder height or slightly higher as it travels forward.

This explanation is very technical, and you won't want to attempt using it with your youngsters. Trust us, Coach, while you're communicating your expertise, the kids will be so bored that they'll start constructing grass huts. An effective way of explaining this concept is to describe this part of the arm movement as being a bit like waving goodbye as the

Figure 4.7   Proper elbow and hand position when snapping the ball toward the target.

arm moves forward. You can also tell the players to pretend that they have a worm on their finger and that they need to fling it off quickly. This analogy usually gets a giggle but also gets the point across. Another analogy you can use to promote accuracy is to have the players make a peace sign with their index and middle fingers. Then have them practice the throwing motion without a ball. Tell them that when they snap to their target, they must cover each eyeball of their target (i.e., the player they are throwing to) with each finger as if they were poking out the eyes of the target.

Follow-Through   For the follow-through, or finish, the back foot should release off the ground (see figure 4.8). If the player does a good job of moving through the ball with the first three steps, then the follow-through will happen automatically. However, when teaching beginners, you will have to remind them to release the back foot. One way to help them remember is to tell them to try to drag the laces of the rear shoe in the grass. The arm should be long and loose after the snap, and it should continue forward and down across the front of the body with the throwing hand finishing by touching the hip or upper thigh on the opposite side of the body.

Figure 4.8   On the follow-through, players must release their back foot.

Putting It All Together   A fun and easy way to help beginners learn the three Ss and the follow-through for proper throwing mechanics is to teach them the Scarecrow Rhyme. The name comes from the fact that the players will get into the same position as a scarecrow to throw the ball. The rhyme speaks directly to what the throwing arm should be doing once the ball is separated from the glove. (See drill 2 on page 81 for more details about implementing the rhyme). Young players usually have fun yelling "Scarecrow!" when they get to the full stretch position.

Scarecrow Rhyme

Secure (securing; pulling the glove in front of the throwing shoulder and meeting the glove with the throwing hand)

Thumb to the thigh (separating; pulling the ball down and back and moving the hand past the throwing-side leg)

Elbows up high (separating; extending both elbows out to the side in a straight line to the target)

Fingers to the sky (separating; moving into the fully stretched position with the throwing hand above the rear elbow)

Scarecrow! (yelled when the players reach the fully stretched position)

Wave bye-bye (snapping)

Drag the laces (following through)

A player should go through the rhyme slowly at first, and she should not go faster until she can get all her joints in the line of force, or in a good scarecrow position. On our teams, the returning players from the previous year often jump with exuberance when we ask, "Does anyone know the Scarecrow Rhyme?" This rhyme may be silly, but it is also fun and effective for teaching the correct mechanics of throwing.

Because throwing is a critical skill, every practice and pregame warm-up should include throwing drills. For players who are at least eight years old, you can teach a throwing progression to help them refine their skills. Drills 3 through 6 in this chapter constitute a throwing progression you can use with players. Don't attempt the progression until players have mastered using the rhyme to execute proper throwing movements, which may take about three or four practices. Using the entire progression for players younger than eight may not be a good idea because they have more limited attention spans. However, that does not mean they cannot do some of the drills individually. For the last three drills (8, 9, and 10), you can have players back up the throws to make the drills proceed more smoothly and to give players in line something to do. The concept of backing up a throw as a defensive strategy is discussed in chapter 7.

Throwing to Make a Play

As your players become more comfortable with throwing, you'll want them to begin working on throwing to specific targets. Infielders will be throwing to first base most of the time because they'll be trying to get the batter-runner out at first. Infielders also need to practice throwing fielded balls to the other bases because in some game situations the throw to another base will be the easiest out. For example, if the bases are loaded and the ball is hit back to the pitcher, she could make an easy throw to the catcher at home plate to get the out.

The outfielders should be preventing the batter-runner from getting an extra base on the hit. So, throwing to second base needs to be automatic, which takes practice. Watch any youth softball game and you'll see that many outfielders do not get the ball back in to the infield quickly. If a young player catches a ball in the outfield, she may be so proud of the accomplishment that she forgets that she needs to throw the ball right away. Don't be surprised to see an outfielder run the ball in to the pitcher from the fence. This may occur if a player is not confident in her arm strength or accuracy.

Drill 1 Zigzag

EQUIPMENT   Bucket of softie balls; empty bucket

PURPOSE   This drill is used to teach receiving skills. The drill also helps players learn one another's names.

PROCEDURE   Have the players line up in two rows facing each other approximately 10 feet (3 m) apart. The players in the two lines (rows) can be staggered or straight across from each other. Place a bucket of balls at one end of the two lines and an empty bucket at the other end. The coach feeds a ball from the bucket to the first player in one line. This player catches the ball, calls out the name of the first player in the other line, and then tosses the ball underhand to that player. The first player in that line calls out the name of the second player in the first line and tosses the ball to her. This action continues down the line; the ball zigzags down the line until it reaches the last player. Each player should catch the ball with her glove hand and should use proper catching technique. Feed additional balls down the line when the previous ball is at the fourth player. The last player tosses the balls into the empty bucket.

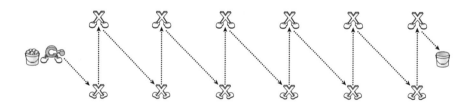

COACHING POINTS   To get players to focus on the play they are making rather than watch the other balls zigzagging down the line, make sure the players tossing the ball call out the name of the player and make eye contact with the player who will receive the toss. Tell the players not to chase any missed balls (there will be many at first) because more balls are coming down the line. Make sure that the players step to the ball with the correct foot when making the catch. Also make sure that their fingers are in the correct position when the ball is caught.

MODIFICATIONS   To start out, have the players do this drill without gloves so they can see the position of their hands. Then, when they put the glove on, the task becomes easier, and the players are better able to manipulate the glove correctly. When your players' throwing skills improve, you can create a competition with this drill. Increase the distance between the lines so the players can throw the ball hard using the correct throwing mechanics. Assign a point for every overthrow or missed catch and challenge the players to get as low a score as possible.

Drill 2 Scarecrow Rhyme

⚾ BEGINNER

EQUIPMENT   A ball for each pair of players

PURPOSE   This drill helps players learn the proper throwing mechanics.

PROCEDURE   Have the players line up in two rows facing each other approximately 15 to 20 feet (4.5 to 6.1 m) apart. This drill is best done in the dirt so you can draw a straight line between each pair of players to represent the line of force. Designate one line (row) of players to start the drill as the throwers. The players in the opposite line partner up with a thrower and should be ready to catch. Each player in the throwing line starts with a ball in her glove. The glove should be stretched out in front of her, and she should place her glove-side foot in front of her and just to the side of the line of force as if she has just caught the ball. The drill progresses when you make the following six commands: *secure, thumb to the thigh, elbows up high, fingers to the sky, wave bye-bye,* and *drag the laces.* On the first 10 reps for each line, have all the players do the rhyme together as the coach gives all the commands; all the balls should be thrown at the same time and in the same direction. The players can do the next 10 to 20 reps at their own speed without the coach giving the commands. For these reps, the players must say the rhyme as they throw.

COACHING POINTS   Make sure the receivers are ready for the ball before you start the drill. Be sure the throwers start the drill with their glove and their glove-side foot in the specified position (as though they have just caught the ball). Regardless of who is saying the commands, whenever players reach the fully stretched position (on "fingers to the sky"), they must yell out "Scarecrow!"

Drill 3 Wrist Snaps

EQUIPMENT   A ball (taped as described on page 70) for each pair of players

PURPOSE   This drill isolates the wrist from the arm in order to help players learn a proper release for throwing.

PROCEDURE   Have the players line up in two rows facing each other approximately 5 feet (152 cm) apart. The players in both lines (rows) should kneel on their throwing knee with their glove-side knee up. The players are not wearing gloves. Each player in the throwing line starts with a ball. These players begin with their throwing arm out in front of them; the elbow of the throwing arm should be bent at 90 degrees so that the upper arm is parallel to the ground. To keep their throwing arm still, players should grab their throwing arm close to the wrist with their nonthrowing hand (see photo). Players hold the ball using a four-seam grip with their middle finger and thumb lined up with the tape. The players snap their wrist forward and their fingers down to release the ball, trying to put as much backspin on the ball as they can. The partners in the receiving line should catch the ball with their nonthrowing hand, quickly bring the ball back to their throwing hand, and then repeat the process, throwing the ball back to their partner.

COACHING POINTS   Kneeling on the ground can be uncomfortable for some players. These players can use their glove as a cushion under their knee. A player's fingers and thumb should point directly to the ground after she releases the ball. When the ball releases from the hand, it's okay if the ball has an arc on it. Be sure the players focus on a proper exchange from the glove hand to the throwing hand.

Drill 4 Figure Eight

◎◎ INTERMEDIATE

EQUIPMENT A ball (taped as described on page 70) for each pair of players

PURPOSE This drill isolates the arm and shoulders from the hips in order to help players learn a proper arm path, shoulder rotation, and release for throwing.

PROCEDURE Have the players line up in two rows facing each other approximately 15 to 20 feet (4.5 to 6.1 m) apart. The players in both lines (rows) kneel on their throwing knee with their glove-side knee up. The players in the throwing line start in the secure position. To begin the movement, they rotate their shoulders so that their throwing shoulder is facing the target (see photo *a*). Then they rotate back so their glove-side shoulder is facing the target (photo *b*). (The moving of the shoulders back and forth is a bit like a figure eight.) During the rotation, the hands stay together with the ball in the glove and the throwing hand on the ball. When the figure eight is completed, the glove-side shoulder should be facing the target. At this point, the players separate the ball from the glove, make the arm circle, and throw the ball to their partner. The players finish by bending over at the waist and letting the throwing hand fall between the legs and brush the grass with the fingertips. The players in the receiving line should catch the ball out in front of them, quickly move to the secure position, and repeat the process.

COACHING POINTS Watch for these two common mistakes and correct them immediately: Players do not turn their shoulders completely when doing the figure eight, and players put their glove hand on their knee and block their upper body from following through. Encourage players to check their throws by watching the black tape on the ball.

Drill 5 Rocking Fire

EQUIPMENT   One ball for each pair of players

PURPOSE   This drill helps players decrease the transfer time between catching a ball and throwing it.

PROCEDURE   Have the players line up in two equal rows facing each other no more than 30 feet (9.1 m) apart. (You'll need to adjust the distance based on the arm strength of your players.) One row starts out as the throwers; each player in this row has a ball. The throwers should place their feet slightly wider than shoulder-width apart with all 10 toes facing the player's partner. The players will throw the ball to their partners without taking the usual steps. As the ball moves past the hip during the arm circle, the player's knees should bend, and her hips and shoulders should rotate so that the glove-side shoulder faces the target (see photo *a*). As the player brings the ball up, her knees will start to straighten to pop her hips as the ball is being thrown overhand (photo *b*). The players receiving the thrown ball should catch the ball out in front of them and then repeat the same motion. Once the players have the drill down to where they are doing the correct mechanics, you can start timing them to see how many times they can throw the ball in 30 seconds.

COACHING POINTS   Make sure the players follow through with their thumb facing the ground and their hand finishing at their glove-side thigh.

Drill 6 Three Step

EQUIPMENT   One ball for each pair of players

PURPOSE   This drill teaches players how to effectively combine footwork with upper body movements for throwing and teaches receiving skills.

PROCEDURE   Have the players line up in two rows facing each other about 20 to 30 feet (6.1 to 9.1 m) apart. One row is the throwing line, and the other is the receiving line. The throwing line feeds the receiving line by tossing the ball to their partners using the correct three-step method. The players in the receiving line must catch the ball and throw it back. The first 10 tosses should be to the center of the receiver, the next 10 to the receiver's right (see photo *a*), and the last 10 to the receiver's left (photo *b*). Once the players in the original throwing line have completed their 30 feeds, the lines switch roles and repeat the process.

COACHING POINTS   Make sure that the players are stepping to the ball with their glove foot to catch it and stepping to their target with the second and third steps. The players should not be focused on how hard or accurate their throws are during this drill. The focus is on the footwork.

MODIFICATIONS   To increase the difficulty level, have the players feed each other ground balls that hop once. These too can be thrown to the middle, left, and right of the receiver.

Drill 7 Relays

EQUIPMENT   Three balls

PURPOSE   This drill helps players practice throwing the ball quickly from the outfield.

PROCEDURE   How much time you spend on this drill depends on the age of the players and whether your opponents are hitting many balls to the outfield yet. Have the players form three equal lines approximately 10 to 15 feet (3.0 to 4.5 m) from each other, starting at the right- or left-field foul line. The players in each line should spread across the outfield so they are approximately 30 to 40 feet (9.1 to 12.2 m) apart. All the players should face the foul line so that they are looking at the back of the girl in front of them. The first player (at the foul line) in each line starts with a ball.

Foul line

When you shout "Go!" the second player in each line (who will receive a throw from the first player) yells "Relay! Relay! Relay!" or "Cut! Cut! Cut!" The thrower uses the audible cue to find the receiver quickly and turns to face her. The first player in each line throws to the next player in her line. The throwing and receiving continues down the line. When the last player in the line catches the ball, she throws it back to the player who just threw it to her, and the ball is relayed back to the first player in line.

COACHING POINTS   When receiving the ball, the players need to turn "glove side" toward their target (unless the ball is thrown too far to their throwing side, in which case they will have to make a complete turn to face their target).

MODIFICATIONS   When players can complete this drill with few mistakes, create a competition between the three lines. The first line to get the ball to the end of the line and back wins. To make sure all players get practice being in the middle of the relay, have the players rotate after completing two relays by calling out "Rotate!" At that command, the first player in line rotates to the second position, the second player to the third position, and so on. The last player in each line sprints to the front of the line and picks up the ball that was left behind by the first player in line; these players then start the next relay.

Drill 8 Around the Horn—Counterclockwise

⚾⚾⚾ ADVANCED

EQUIPMENT Bucket of balls

PURPOSE This drill helps players learn the proper footwork for throwing the ball to the right and increases their communication skills.

PROCEDURE Have players form four equal lines on the bases. The first player in each line should be on the base, ready to receive the ball. The other players should be in line behind the first player and should be ready to rotate in. You or an assistant coach should be on the pitcher's mound with a bucket of balls. The coach on the mound starts the drill by throwing a ball to the player at home plate. Moving counterclockwise, the first player in each line throws a ball to the first player in line at the next base. The girls waiting in line should yell where to throw the ball next, and they should position themselves to back up the receiver. After throwing the ball, each player rotates to the back of the line at the same base. If an overthrow occurs, you can throw a ball from the bucket to keep things moving, or you can have the player who backs up the base throw the ball to the next base. One complete rotation is finished when the player who started at home plate is up again. Continue this drill for four or five rotations.

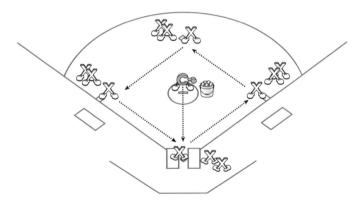

COACHING POINTS Watch for correct three-step mechanics. Also make sure that all the players are backing up their bases, communicating where the ball should be thrown to next, and encouraging each other.

MODIFICATIONS To make this drill easier for younger players, use a parent helper at each base to tell the girls where to throw the ball next. When the players can complete rotations without errors, start keeping time to challenge them. You can also tell players not to retrieve any balls that are overthrown and that get past the backup player. Then you can count them and challenge the girls to keep this number as small as possible.

Drill 9 Around the Horn—Clockwise

EQUIPMENT   Bucket of balls

PURPOSE   This drill helps players learn the proper footwork for throwing the ball to the left and increases their communication skills.

PROCEDURE   Have players form four equal lines on the bases. The first player in each line should be on the base, ready to receive the ball. The others should be in line and should be ready to rotate in. You or an assistant coach should be on the pitcher's mound with a bucket of balls. The coach on the mound starts the drill by throwing a ball to the player at home plate. Beginning at home plate and moving clockwise, the first player in each line throws a ball to the first player in line at the next base. The girls waiting in line should yell where to throw the ball next, and they should position themselves to back up the receiver. After throwing the ball, each player rotates to the back of the line at the same base. If an overthrow occurs, you can throw a ball from the bucket to keep things moving, or you can have the player who backs up the base throw the ball to the next base. One complete rotation is finished when the player who started at home plate is up again. Continue the drill for four or five rotations. The first goal for the players is to throw the ball around the horn without any overthrown or missed balls.

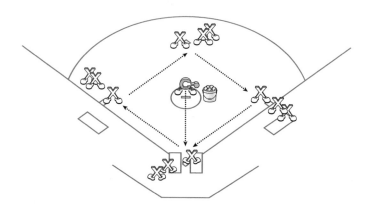

COACHING POINTS Watch for correct three-step mechanics. Also make sure that all the players are backing up their bases, communicating where to throw next, and encouraging each other.

MODIFICATIONS For beginning players, use a parent helper at each base to tell the girls where to throw the ball next. When the players can complete rotations without errors, start keeping time to challenge them further. You can also ask players to leave any balls that are overthrown or that get past the backup player; at the end of the drill, you can count these balls and challenge the girls to keep this number low.

Drill 10 Around the Horn—Star

EQUIPMENT   Bucket of balls

PURPOSE   This drill helps players learn proper footwork.

PROCEDURE   This drill starts the same as drills 8 and 9; the players are evenly distributed at each base. For this version, the throwing sequence will be from home to second, second to first, first to third, and third to home. After throwing the ball, the players will rotate counterclockwise, sprinting to the end of the line at the next base (from home to first, to second, to third, then home). The coach starts the drill by throwing a ball to the first player in line at home plate. This player starts the "star" by throwing to second base. She then sprints to first base and goes to the back of the line. Every player will rotate to the next base after she throws the ball. The rotation is complete when the player who started the drill reaches home, gets to the front of the line again, and catches the ball. The first goal for the players is to throw the ball around the horn without any overthrown or missed balls. If an overthrown ball gets past the backup player, you can throw a ball from the bucket to keep things moving. If the backup player gets the ball, she should throw it to the next base.

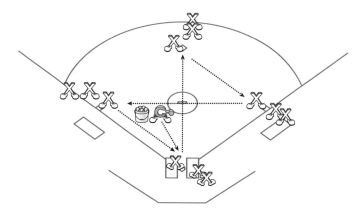

COACHING POINTS   Watch for correct three-step mechanics. Also make sure that all the players are backing up their bases, communicating where to throw next, and encouraging each other. Sprinting to each base will help players improve their conditioning.

MODIFICATIONS   To make this drill easier for younger players, position a parent helper at each base to tell the girls where to throw the ball next. When players get comfortable with the drill, you can start keeping time to add a challenge. You can also challenge your players to keep overthrows and balls that get past the backup player to a minimum.

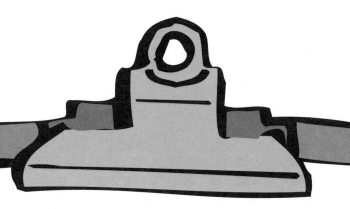

The Coach's Clipboard

✔ Use tennis balls, sponge balls, or softie balls when young players are first learning to throw and catch.

✔ Proper catching mechanics include moving to the ball with the glove-side foot and having the fingers pointed to the sky when receiving the ball above the waist or having the fingers pointed to the ground when receiving the ball below the waist.

✔ Throwing mechanics for the upper body consist of the three Ss (secure, separate, and snap) and the follow-through.

✔ Throwing mechanics for the lower body consist of three steps: glove-side foot steps to the outside of the ball's path, throwing-side foot steps past the glove-side foot, and glove-side foot steps toward the target.

✔ The line of force, or power line, is the direct line between the thrower and the target. Players must learn to align their major joints with the line of force.

✔ Throwing drills should be incorporated into every practice and pregame warm-up.

Teaching Fielding Skills With 10 Simple Drills

Most youngsters know that on defense they will need to stop the ball and throw to the base that a runner is running to. They also know that the ball must get to the base before the runner does in order to get the out. However, knowing what to do and actually doing it are two different things. After three innings of watching grasshoppers bouncing by her position, your left fielder may not be paying attention when the batter cracks one her way—and before you know it, all chaos breaks loose. Suddenly, coaches, parents, and complete strangers are yelling at her: "Get the ball!" If you are lucky, she will wake up from her daydream and go get the ball. But more often than not, the fielder from center field runs over and grabs the ball, adding insult to injury. Of course, keeping kids focused is only half the battle. Even if the fielder is paying attention and smacking her glove in anticipation, things can still go awry when a slow roller comes directly at her. She may be waiting in a good fielding position, and then right as the ball gets to her, she might turn or lift her head and let the ball go right between her legs.

These situations may make you want to tear your hair out. To avoid doing so, you simply need to keep things in perspective. Players all the way up to the pro level "fall asleep" and make mistakes; they just don't do it as often. If older players and professionals can foul up on occasion, you'll have to accept that your beginners are sometimes going to zone out during a game. This chapter provides information that will help you teach your players how to focus, how to physically set up for the ball, and how to field ground balls and fly balls hit to them.

Focus

For youth players, being mentally prepared for the ball is about 90 percent of the battle to successfully field a ball. In leagues for players under eight years old, most batted balls will not be traveling fast enough to hurt or get by the fielders. When fielders miss a hit ball, it is usually because they were not paying attention or because they were not in the correct position to successfully field the ball.

In the first defensive practice, let the players know that you do not expect them to be focusing hard during the entire game. Tell them that you will only ask for five seconds of hard focus from the start of every pitch. For these five seconds, the defensive players need to step into their "circle of focus." The circle of focus is two things. First, it is the spot on the field that the defender is playing. And second, it is the place mentally where the defender is thinking about nothing except expecting the ball to be hit to her and knowing where she is going to throw the ball after she has fielded it. After the pitch is delivered or the play has finished, the players can step out of the circle of focus and relax (or wave at mom, chase butterflies, or continue to build a grass hut in the outfield). Sometimes you will need to remind the players that the pitcher is ready to pitch by using key words such as "circle of focus" or "five seconds." On hearing these words, the players should pop back into the game and start to prepare mentally and physically for the ball to be hit to them.

To help young or beginning players learn this concept, you can actually draw a circle on the field where their position is to be played. For instance, the second-base player will be positioned halfway between first and second base, just in front of or just behind the baseline. Draw a circle in the dirt in this area. Then explain to the player that when she steps into this circle, she must start to look at the pitcher and the batter. Tell her that she needs to be in a good fielding position when the pitcher delivers the pitch.

Make sure the players understand that when the pitcher steps on the rubber, the defenders must step into their circle, start to focus on the play, and think about where they need to throw the ball if it is hit to them. When the pitcher starts her motion, the five seconds of hard focus starts, and the defenders must get into a ready position, expecting the ball to be hit to them. When practicing this concept, have an assistant pretend to pitch to you at home plate. This will enable you to see if the players are actually getting ready and stepping into their circles. Once the players understand that this method is getting them mentally prepared for the ball, you can move on to teaching the players how to get physically prepared for a ball that is hit to them.

Setup Positions

To be prepared physically for the ball, the defensive players need to be in a good setup position when the ball is hit. The exact setup position differs for the various positions on the field, but in general, the defenders should start with a good athletic position that includes flexion in the ankles, knees, and hips. Their hands need to be out in front of them ready for the ball. Their weight should be shifted slightly forward as the pitched ball is traveling to the batter, which will put them on the balls of their feet.

All fielders will take a small step forward with their glove-side foot, landing it just as the ball reaches the batter. This is referred to as the contact step. The contact step gets the fielder moving at the time that the ball is to be hit by the batter. This step provides two main benefits for the fielder: The fielder is able to read the ball off the bat faster, and the fielder has a foot to push off of when taking her first step to the ball. The contact step is critical for players to maximize their first-step quickness to the ball. Without the contact step, the players would have to start out from a static (resting) position to move to the ball rather than a dynamic (moving) position.

Just as when practicing getting in and out of the circle of focus, you should again have an assistant on the mound simulating pitches to you at home plate so you can check your players physical preparedness to receive the ball. As with batting in chapter 3, the MCP cadence can help defensive players prepare to receive the ball. You can account for the contact step by adding on to the cadence and making it motion-critical-pitch-contact. As the pitcher starts the motion, the players should get into a good athletic position. When the pitcher strides forward (critical), the players bring their hands out in front of them, getting ready to receive the ball. When the pitcher releases the ball, the players should start shifting their weight forward and then take a small step (the contact step) toward the batter with their glove-side foot just as the ball passes by the batter. When the ball has been caught by the catcher, the defenders can stand up and relax. Table 5.1 shows the relationship between the movements of the pitcher and those of the fielder.

Table 5.1   Fielder Responses to the MCP Cadence

Cadence	Pitcher	Fielder
Motion	Starts the windup	Assumes a good athletic position with flexed knees, ankles, and waist
Critical	Begins to stride forward	Brings the hands out in front
Pitch	Releases the ball	Shifts onto the balls of the feet and creeps forward

When running drills, coaches sometimes let the players start slacking on their setup position. This occurs because the coach is trying to get more reps in or because the coach wants to keep the players moving so they don't get distracted. However, you should take the time at the beginning of each drill to make sure the players are in the correct setup position before continuing. This will help ensure that the setup becomes second nature to the players. During the drills, you may notice that some young players have a tendency not to spread their feet apart as they bend their knees. At first, they may resemble a ballerina more than a softball player. But keep working with them and be patient.

Position for Corners

As a general rule, the closer a defensive player is to the batter, the more she needs to look like a catcher. The catcher is usually in a full squatted position very low to the ground. Her glove is extended straight out in front of her with a slight bend in her elbow. The fingers of the glove hand are pointed up, and the palm is facing away toward the pitcher, waiting to receive the pitch. (See chapter 6 for more information about the proper position for the catcher.) The catcher's throwing hand will be behind her back to keep it away from foul tips and wild pitches.

The corners, or the first- and third-base players, can be positioned anywhere from 3 to 15 feet (91 cm to 4.5 m) in front of first base and third base, putting them about 45 to 57 feet (13.7 to 17.4 m) from the batter. Because of their close proximity to the batter, the corners should use a modified catcher's position. The corners need to be prepared for "hot shots," or hard-hit balls coming directly at them. They must cover a lot of ground in front of them to field bunts and little dribbling hits, which are very common in youth softball.

The corners will not be in a full squat like the catcher, but they will have about a 90-degree bend in their knees. Their feet should be just beyond shoulder-width apart, and their hands need to be out in front of them (see figure 5.1).

Figure 5.1   Proper setup position for corner players (first- and third-base players).

Position for Middle Fielders

The middle fielders, the shortstop and the second-base defender, are typically positioned about 65 to 75 feet (19.8 to 22.8 m) from the batter. These players have more time to react to the ball than the corners do, and they must cover more ground laterally. Because the middle fielders must be able to move quickly in all directions, they need to be in a more upright athletic position. This position should resemble a basketball defender or a tennis player receiving the ball.

The defender's knees should be bent to about 45 degrees, and the feet should be approximately shoulder-width apart (see figure 5.2). Both the glove hand and the throwing hand are extending out and down in front of the defender; the elbows are slightly bent, the fingers are facing

Figure 5.2   Proper setup position for middle infielders (shortstop and second-base player).

slightly downward, and the palm is facing toward the batter (almost as if she is shaking hands with someone). The throwing hand of the middle fielders will be extended out just short of the glove hand. This is to make sure that the glove comes in contact with the ball first.

Position for Outfielders

Outfielders are the last line of defense for keeping a batter from getting extra bases on a hit. Although outfielders will not need to react as fast as infielders to a hit ball, they still need to be in an athletic position when the ball is pitched. Outfielders are expected to stop all balls within five paces in any direction. Outfielders should have a slight bend in their knees and their feet shoulder-width apart (see figure 5.3). They will not need to bend their knees as far as the middle infielders do, but they should not have straight legs. The outfielders can position their hands at about waist level with their fingers facing slightly downward and their hands extended out from their body and down.

Figure 5.3 Proper setup position for outfielders.

Fielding a Ground Ball

Various methods are used for teaching players how to field a ground ball. Unfortunately, several of those methods are ineffective. One ineffective method is hitting ground balls to the players where they stand. This leads the players to expect that they will not have to move to field a ball. Another ineffective approach is to hit ground balls continuously to seven-year-olds who do not know how to field a ball. They will fail over and over again; you'll be frustrated, and they may be terrified. New players are often so scared of the ball that they look as if they are running away from a tyrannosaur.

One popular technique that many coaches teach requires the fielder to move in front of the ball, get into a setup position, and wait to receive the ball to her center. The fielder tips her head down so the coach or batter can see the button on top of her hat or so her ponytail flips forward over the top of her head. When coaches are teaching this method, you may hear them use phrases such as "Let me see the button of your hat," "Use soft hands," and "Ponytail flip." This technique may work for baseball because the ball is smaller and the basepaths are 90 feet, giving the fielder a little more time to field the ball. However, this technique is simply too slow for softball. The 60-foot basepaths in softball require players to field the ball quickly.

In softball, a better technique is for the fielder to be in motion just before the ball is put into play. When players field the ball, their movement should be continuous from the time the ball touches the glove until the ball is thrown. Players can achieve this fluidity by moving to the ball and through the ball. They should field the ball in front of their body between their glove-side foot and the center of their body. Players need to keep their head up so they can still see the field with their peripheral vision and so they can get the ball to their throwing shoulder quickly. This method allows the players to transition quickly to throwing the ball.

The key to successfully fielding balls in the infield is for players to move to the ball and not wait for the ball to get to them. You do not want players trying to stand their ground and not moving to the ball at all. After the contact step that players take when the ball reaches the batter, the next step players should take is called the crossover step. When the fielder needs to move right or left, the step will be a crossover step to either side (see figure 5.4). If the ball is hit short of the player or over the fielder's head, the crossover step may actually be a forward step (made without hesitation) or a drop step back. The crossover step allows fielders to cover more ground and get to the ball more quickly. The purpose of the crossover step is to enable players to get to the ball before it gets to them so that they can have their body in front of the ball path before they field it.

Players may need to take more than one step to move into the proper position. Any footwork needed between the contact step and the first throwing step (the step taken during the securing component of a throw; see chapter 4) should be performed as quickly as possible so fielders move from fielding the ball to making the throw in as little time as possible. You can refer to this concept as *first-step quickness*. This will help remind players that they need to move to get to the ball and then keep

Figure 5.4   After the contact step (taken as the ball meets the bat), an infielder should take a crossover step to move into position so her body is in front of the ball path.

moving through the play all the way to the throw. This strategy will also help them remember that throwing is simply an extension of fielding the ball.

In addition to practicing footwork, you need to work on the arm movement for fielding the ball. A common pitfall in fielding is when players bend at the waist, look down, and stab down at the ball with their glove. This can allow the ball to roll right under the glove if the fielder's timing isn't perfect. And guess what, it won't be. A better approach is to tell each player to bring her glove down to the ground and land it like an airplane on a runway—not like a helicopter landing on a pad. When fielders land their glove like an airplane, they must squat down to keep their eyes looking forward.

When the fielder steps forward with her glove-side foot (the first step for throwing), she should bring her glove to the ground and scoop up some dirt (see figure 5.5). She should make a 2- to 4-inch (5.1 to 10.2 cm) mark on the ground as she pushes her glove forward in the dirt. During this motion, her weight should be on the balls of her feet. Players will often miss a routine slow-rolling ground ball when their weight is on their heels. This position causes the glove to come off the ground right before the ball gets there. If the fielder moves forward with the first step and gets into the right body position, the chance of the ball going under the glove decreases dramatically. Pushing their glove through the dirt helps players learn that they need to push their glove through the ball as they are stepping forward.

For outfielders, the technique for fielding a ground ball is a little different from the technique for infielders. When fielding a ground ball that has gotten past the infield, the outfielder completes the same movements as an infielder up to and including stepping to the outside of the path of the ball with the glove-side foot. However, instead of landing their glove through the ball, outfielders should drop their glove-side knee to the ground sideways to block the ball in case it gets past their glove (see figure 5.6). They should not try to scoop the ball like an infielder. Instead, they should point their fingers straight down and use the glove to block the ball. This is a great technique to teach beginners because it will decrease the odds of the ball getting past them.

Figure 5.5 When fielding a ground ball, an infield player should have her weight on the balls of her feet. She should bring her glove to the ground and then move it forward through the ball.

After infielders or outfielders have successfully caught the ball in their glove, they should bring the glove up to just below their throwing shoulder to secure the ball with their throwing hand. They will then continue with the usual procedure for throwing the ball (as described in chapter 4). The transition from fielding to throwing involves securing the ball with the throwing hand while the glove and ball are being taken to the throwing side of the body. This transition makes throwing a seamless extension of fielding the ball.

Keep in mind that beginning players will not be able to execute proper fielding technique if you just explain the principles of the technique to them.

Figure 5.6 When fielding a ground ball, an outfielder should drop her glove-side knee to the ground.

You will need to help them burn in good muscle memory. You can do this by performing drills that help the players learn the steps, and feeding balls to the players in a nonthreatening manner (such as soft tossing or placing the ball into the glove). The drills at the end of this chapter will help give your players the practice they need. When you first add live balls, the fielding practice may look like a yoga class gone amuck. But stick with it, Coach. After implementing these principles, our team went from committing 25 fielding errors during a tournament to limiting the errors to 5 in the course of six games.

Fielding a Fly Ball

For seven- or eight-year-olds, catching a fly ball may be the most frightful thing they have ever done. Therefore, you need to be patient with your younger players. Helping them get in front of a ball and keep it from going past them will be a step in the right direction.

Some coaches subscribe to the principle that an outfielder's first movement needs to be back, not forward. When we first started coaching, we followed this principle too. Unfortunately, this principle contradicts the principle that defensive players need to be in motion when the ball is hit. The contradicting messages resulted in players hesitating and not moving at all. By observing top athletes in the game, we realized that outfielders and infielders move the same way. They take a contact step as the ball reaches the batter. They read the ball during this step, and then they move to the ball quickly with a crossover step. This method is much easier for players to understand, and it enables them to get to the ball more quickly. When a ball is hit over their head, outfielders will use a drop step—meaning that their left or right foot will drop behind them—but this step occurs after the contact step. As noted on page 99, the drop step is used as a crossover step when needed.

You will probably rotate some players from the infield to the outfield during games (which is a good practice). After playing the infield, a player's first reaction will be to explode forward when the ball is hit. So, don't be surprised if lots of balls end up going over the outfielders' heads. If this occurs, don't sweat it, Coach. Much worse things could happen. If a fielder moves in any direction to try to get the ball, you should count that as a success because it means that she got into her circle of focus.

The biggest hurdle you'll face in teaching your players to catch fly balls is preventing them from holding their gloves like baskets (with their palms up). The proper technique for catching a fly ball is with the fingers pointed up and back (see figure 5.7). Players should also catch the ball in front of them, just above their eyes. To reinforce this technique, tell the players to get their nose under the ball and to catch the ball in front of their face. The glove hand and the throwing hand should be in front of the player and below her line of sight to the ball; the hands should never be above the fielder's head. The glove should be moving up and forward to meet the ball. The movement of the glove should resemble an airplane taking off from the airport, not a rocket moving straight up. The throwing hand should be off to the side and below the glove to assist in catching the ball; this posi-

tion also allows for a quick transfer of the ball to the throwing hand. If you want to avoid calling the ambulance, you should introduce this skill using sponge balls or water balloons. After the players have confidence in catching a ball above their nose, you may introduce the type of ball that will be used during a game.

The hardest skill for your five- to seven-year-old outfielders to master will be catching balls that are hit over their heads. The good news, Coach, is that not too many five- to seven-year-olds can hit a ball this far. To make the catch, the outfielder needs to catch the ball on the run. She should run, pumping her arms, and time the catch by stretching out her glove hand in time to catch the ball while in stride. This kind of catch looks similar to a catch made by a football wide receiver.

Figure 5.7 Proper technique for catching a fly ball.

Drill 1 First-Step Quickness

🌑 BEGINNER

EQUIPMENT Two cones; two softballs

PURPOSE This drill gives players practice in performing the contact step and assuming the proper position to field a ball.

PROCEDURE Set up two cones a couple feet apart. Place one softball in front of each cone and one softball a few steps to the outside of each cone. Players form a line behind each cone. The first player in each line steps to the outside of her line's cone so that she is positioned between the two balls. You or an assistant coach should stand behind and between the cones, facing the players. When you yell "Contact!" both players assume the contact step position. When the players are in the proper position, you point to the balls, and the players take a crossover step and any additional steps that are needed to reach the ball. The first player to get to the ball and pick it up wins. These two players move to the end of their line, and the next two players go. You can keep score to see which line wins.

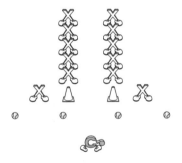

COACHING POINTS The emphasis here should be on quickness. If your players need some additional incentive to move as quickly as possible, try replacing the balls with candy. Players have to be the first to pick up the candy if they want to keep it.

Drill 2 Glove Work

BEGINNER

EQUIPMENT None

PURPOSE This drill is used to teach proper fielding technique.

PROCEDURE Have the players line up in two rows facing the same direction. The coach stands in front of the rows, facing the players. The coach yells "Contact!" to signal the players to get in a contact step position and get ready to move. When the coach points over the shoulder and to the rear, the players take two steps forward, starting with the foot on the throwing side. As the glove-side foot hits the ground, the players lower their gloves and push the tip of their gloves through the dirt, making a 2- to 4-inch (5.1 to 10.2 cm) mark in the dirt (see photo). The players continue the proper footwork (step with the throwing-side foot and then step to the target with the glove-side foot) to get into a throwing position and then return to the starting position.

COACHING POINTS Check to make sure the players are starting in a good athletic position. The players should land their gloves like an airplane. Be sure to correct any players who are bending over at the waist and landing the glove like a helicopter.

MODIFICATIONS Once the players are using the correct footwork and posture for fielding a ball in front of them, the coach can point to the left or right to indicate a ball coming to the players to either side. The players will need to perform a crossover step to the side indicated by the coach; they will then take the step to field the ball on the ground. When the players move to their throwing side, make sure they do not backhand the ball by turning their glove over, and make sure they aren't fielding the ball to the side of their body. As with balls moving right at them, the players should move so that they can field the ball between the glove-side foot and the center of their body, keeping their glove facing forward and up.

Drill 3 MCPC Cadence

EQUIPMENT None

PURPOSE This drill helps players learn the proper mental and physical preparation for fielding a ball.

PROCEDURE Have the players line up in two rows. Both rows of players should be facing the same direction. Position yourself out in front of the players. You should face the same direction as the players so they can easily mimic your movements. Call out the commands of the MCPC cadence, stopping at each of the four stages of getting ready to field a ball:

- *Motion.* Coach and players assume a good athletic position.
- *Critical.* Coach and players bring their hands out in front of them.
- *Pitch.* Coach and players start shifting their weight forward on to the balls of their feet.
- *Contact.* Coach and players take a small step forward with the glove-side foot.

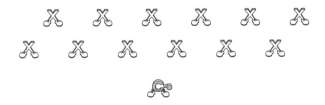

COACHING POINTS Consider having an assistant coach lead this drill. This will allow you to walk around and make sure that each player is assuming the correct position for each command.

MODIFICATIONS Once the players have the movements down, the coach can pitch the ball to an assistant, and the players should cue their positions to the pitching movement. The coach should continue to call out the commands: *motion* to start the windup, *critical* on the stride, *pitch* on the release. On *contact,* the assistant will need to swing. When your players have the basic cadence down, you can add additional movement. After the contact command, the coach points to the left, to the right, to the front (for moving forward), or over the shoulder and to the rear (for moving to the backward), and the players take two steps in the direction indicated.

Drill 4 Feeds

⚾ BEGINNER

EQUIPMENT   Bucket of balls

PURPOSE   This drill helps players learn the correct mechanics of fielding; more advanced players can also work on their quickness.

PROCEDURE   Have players line up at the pitcher's mound. You should be positioned about 5 feet (152 cm) in front and to the side of the line with a bucket of balls. A second coach or a parent should be at home plate. You will soft toss a ball so it lands about 3 feet (91 cm) in front of the first player in line. Use the MCPC cadence to help players time their movements. When you show the ball in your outstretched hand, the fielder should enter her circle of focus. When you lift the ball up (motion), the fielder gets into a good athletic stance. Swing the ball down to below your waist, pausing at the bottom of the arc (critical), and then release the ball (pitch) so that it bounces far enough in front of the fielder that she has to step to the ball. The contact step should be timed to occur when the ball first hits the ground. Then the player steps forward and tries to field the ball on the bounce before it hits the ground again. After fielding the ball, the player throws the ball to the coach at home plate, and then rotates to the end of the line.

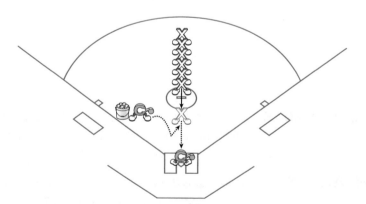

COACHING POINTS   Make sure the players are getting their butt down when fielding the ball. Don't allow players to just bend over at the waist to get to the ball. Players should watch the ball all the way into the glove, then look up to find their target as they bring the glove to their throwing shoulder.

MODIFICATIONS   The first time you introduce this drill, you can have the players catch the ball in the air while they are stepping forward. Do this for the first couple of reps so the players get used to the movement before you add in the fielding. When the players can do the drill correctly, you can move farther in front of them and toss the ball from a farther distance. Eventually, you can feed balls down the middle, to the left, and to the right. As the players advance, you can increase the challenge by moving the line back to second base. You can also move the other coach to first or third base so the players have to throw to the right and left. You may start throwing the ball instead of soft tossing, but don't do this until the players have mastered coming through the ball.

Drill 5 Cross Lines

EQUIPMENT   Two buckets of balls; two empty buckets; two bats

PURPOSE   This drill helps players learn to field batted ground balls.

PROCEDURE   Divide the players into two groups; one group forms a line at the second-base position, and the other group forms a line at the shortstop position. Place an empty bucket at the rear of each line. The coach and an assistant are positioned at home plate with two buckets of balls. One of the coaches is on the first-base side of home plate, and the other coach is on the third-base side. The coach on the first-base side will be hitting ground balls to the line of players at the shortstop position; the coach on the third-base side will be hitting ground balls to the line of players at the second-base position. The first player in each line fields the hit ball and returns to the back of the line, dropping the fielded ball into the bucket. The coaches need to time the hits so the balls do not collide. For the drill to work best, the hits should be one right after the other. When a coach's bucket is empty, replace it with the bucket of balls from the fielding line.

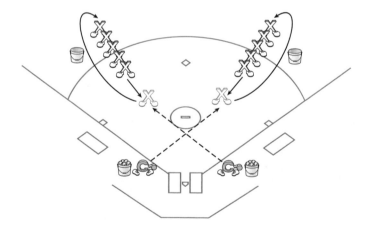

COACHING POINTS When starting this drill, hit easy ground balls directly at the players. After a few rotations through the lines, hit the balls to the left and to the right. The key is to avoid hitting the ball so hard that the players stand back and wait for the ball to get to them. If you see this happen, then hit the ball softer, forcing the players to come forward to the ball. Reacting forward to the ball should become second nature for the players; however, this might take an entire season of hitting balls softly to them.

MODIFICATIONS As the players become more confident in their fielding skills, you can create an elimination game from this drill. In this version, you run the drill as described, but if a player misfields a ball in any manner (not coming through the ball, bobbling the ball, or just missing it), she is eliminated and must sit out until the round is over. The last player standing in each line will compete against each other. You can determine your own rewards for winning, such as receiving an ice cream coupon or an extra treat at the end of practice.

Drill 6 Shortstop Hole

EQUIPMENT Bucket of balls; bat

PURPOSE This drill gives players practice in fielding and throwing from the shortstop position; players also practice throwing to all the bases.

PROCEDURE One player is positioned at shortstop, one player at home plate, and one player at each base. The remaining players line up at third base and wait to rotate in. You stand on the first-base side of home plate with a bucket of balls. You will hit five ground balls to the shortstop. The shortstop throws the first two to first base. The first-base player fires the ball to the player covering home (figure a). The shortstop throws the third ground ball to the second-base player, who throws the ball to the first-base player, who throws it to home (figure b). The shortstop throws the fourth ground ball to the third-base player, who throws the ball to home (figure c). The last ground ball is thrown home by the shortstop. After the shortstop makes her last throw, the players rotate: The first player in the line moves to third base. The player at third moves to shortstop; shortstop to second; second to first; and first to the catcher position. The former catcher goes to the back of the line at third. Continue the drill until each player has moved through the entire rotation.

COACHING POINTS This drill is the transition drill where players begin to combine the throwing skills with the fielding skills. Because throwing is an extension of fielding, this drill is just the natural progression for teaching the proper mechanics of fielding a ball and throwing to a base. The goal is to have the player field the ball correctly and then throw to a target quickly. Watch to make sure that players continue to use the correct mechanics to field the ball. They should be coming to the ball and through it as they are fielding, and they should continue to step toward the base they are throwing to.

MODIFICATIONS After the players have gone through one rotation, you can hit ground balls to the second-base position, then the third-base position, and so on. You can also have an assistant coach use a stopwatch to time the players' throws to first. The time starts when the ball first touches the fielder's glove and stops when the ball hits the glove of the target. This is known as glove-to-glove time, and it usually refers to the time it takes a catcher to throw the ball to second base once she receives the pitch. However, you can use the measurement in this drill to encourage all the players to transition from fielding to throwing quickly.

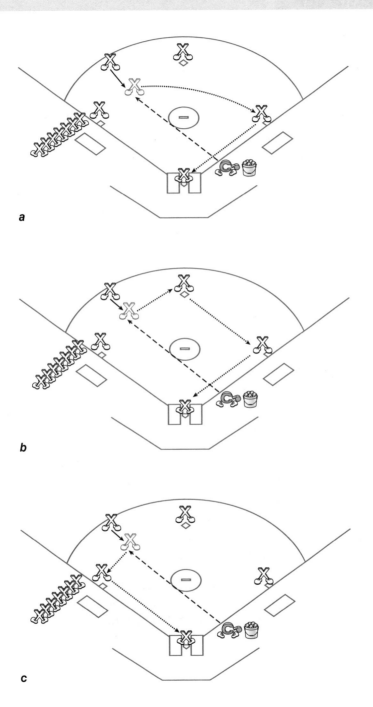

a

b

c

Drill 7 Self-Toss

EQUIPMENT   A softie ball for each player (softballs can be used later)

PURPOSE   This drill teaches players to get under the ball when fielding fly balls.

PROCEDURE   Give each player a ball. Have the players spread out on the field so that they will have enough room to toss their ball 10 to 15 feet (3.0 to 4.5 m) in the air and catch it without hitting other players. To start out, all the players will toss the ball up in the air (using an underhand toss) on the coach's command. After a few reps, the players can toss the ball on their own (this will enable them to get in more reps).

COACHING POINTS   Players should catch the ball at the height of the forehead and about 12 to 18 inches (30.5 to 45.7 cm) out in front of the body. Remind players to line up their nose with the ball to get under the ball. This will force them to move their feet and catch the ball above their shoulders. You will see two common errors in this drill: players extending their arms straight up and trying to catch the ball directly above their head and players catching the ball below their shoulders while holding their hands with fingers pointed down. When they catch the ball below their shoulders, their hands will be positioned as if they were holding a bowl of soup. This incorrect technique is the result of players trying to catch the ball too far out in front of them.

MODIFICATIONS   Two competitions can be incorporated into this drill. Players can compete to see how high they can throw the ball and still catch it, or they can compete to see how many times they can catch the ball in succession.

Drill 8 Quick Five

EQUIPMENT   A ball

PURPOSE   This drill helps players learn to move quickly to the ball and get into the proper position to catch a fly ball; players also practice sprinting while wearing a softball glove.

PROCEDURE   Have players line up in two rows about 10 feet (3 m) apart in the outfield (one row behind the other). Both rows of players are facing you. You will give the MCPC cadence with a ball in your hand. You point the ball to the left or right to indicate a fly ball above the players' heads coming to that side. After their contact step, the players drop back to the left or right, depending on which way you point. They turn their hips and take five quick steps at a 45-degree angle, starting with a crossover step. When they get to the fifth step, they should plant their feet, turn back toward you, and simulate catching a ball above their shoulders. Then they should step toward you and simulate a throw. Players then return to their starting position, and the drill is repeated. Complete five reps in both directions.

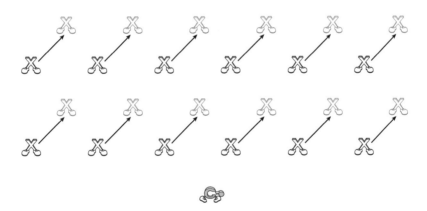

COACHING POINTS   The five steps must be a burst. Make sure the players pump their elbows when running. Players should not hold their glove stretched out in front of them (stiff-armed) as they run.

MODIFICATIONS   As the players get good at dropping back, adjust your pointing directions. Point the ball straight above your head to simulate a pop fly coming straight at the players, which will require them to move straight back. Point the ball down to simulate a ground ball hit to the outfield. The players should respond by stepping forward and not dropping back. The players should simulate catching or fielding the ball in the outfield and then quickly throwing the ball in.

Drill 9 Outfield Feeds

◎◎ INTERMEDIATE

EQUIPMENT   Bucket of balls

PURPOSE   This drill allows players to practice catching fly balls.

PROCEDURE   Players form a line in center field. The coach is positioned at second base with a bucket of balls. The first player in line steps forward, and the coach feeds her a pop-up, using the MCPC cadence to prepare her for the pop-up. The coach tosses the ball approximately five steps from the fielder so she has to move to the ball to catch it. After the catch, the player sprints around the coach and drops the ball in the bucket. The player then returns to the back of the line, and the next player goes. The coach should throw the balls to the right of the player the first time through the line, to the left of the player the second time through, and to the rear of the player the third time through. Continue the drill until each player has the opportunity to catch a ball tossed in each direction.

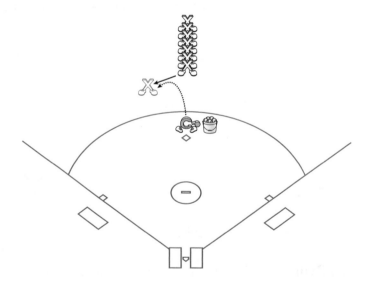

COACHING POINTS   Be sure you feed the balls high enough so the players have enough time to get to the ball and to get into the correct position to catch the ball. Feed the ball to the spot where the players should be after taking the five quick steps. Be careful that the players don't automatically start sprinting forward when you give them these feeds. A player's first motion should be a contact step, and she should read where the ball is going before she takes her five quick steps.

MODIFICATIONS   If only one coach is feeding the balls, this can be a time-consuming drill, and players may be standing around for a long time. If possible, set up more coaches at the edge of the grass tossing to separate lines of players. You can also include feeds to the front of the players so that they have to run up on the ball to catch it.

Drill 10 Defensive Back

EQUIPMENT A bucket of softie balls or small footballs

PURPOSE This drill allows players to practice catching a ball over the shoulder and on the run.

PROCEDURE The coach is positioned at second base facing the outfield. Players form a line next to the coach. The first player in line moves to the outfield grass and faces the coach. The coach tosses the ball moderately high and to a spot that is about five quick steps to the rear of the player. On the throw, the player moves and catches the ball over her shoulder before going to the end of the line. For the first 10 reps, have the players catch the ball with their bare hands. Then switch to using gloves.

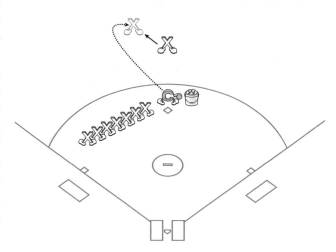

COACHING POINTS Starting out with bare hands helps the players pump their elbows properly when running to get to the ball. For a player to cover ground quickly to the rear, she must turn her hips toward the direction she wants to run. This should eliminate backpedaling and keep the players from looking like gymnasts doing a tumbling routine.

MODIFICATIONS This drill can also be done using footballs. Try to lead the player as best you can by throwing the football out in front of her so that she has to continue to run to catch the ball. If you don't have the arm or accuracy, you may ask a parent or assistant coach to do the throwing. You could also use Frisbees instead of footballs. The nice thing about Frisbees is that they will float and move, requiring the player to constantly keep her eye on the Frisbee. To make it more fun, have two lines of players and two coaches (one for each line). The coaches should throw at the same time. The first line to catch 10 Frisbees wins the competition.

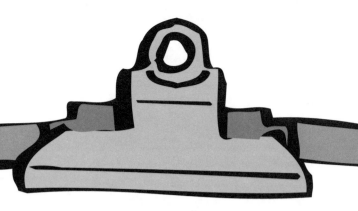

The Coach's Clipboard

✔ Ask young players for five seconds of focus on each pitch.

✔ The motion-critical-pitch-contact cadence is a useful tool for helping defensive players prepare for the ball to be hit to them.

✔ Defensive players achieve first-step quickness by using a crossover step (after the contact step) in the direction of the ball.

✔ Balls should be fielded between the center of the body and the glove-side foot whenever possible.

✔ Outfielders should drop their glove-side knee to the ground to block the path of the ball.

✔ On a ground ball, the movement of the fielder's glove should resemble an airplane landing on the runway, not a helicopter landing on a pad.

✔ Throwing is an extension of fielding; there should not be a pause between fielding a ball and throwing it.

✔ Players should catch fly balls above the shoulders and in front of the body, with their fingers pointed upward.

Teaching Pitching and Catching Skills With 10 Simple Drills

Oh, the hands will go up when you ask, "Can anybody pitch?" Soon girls' arms will be winding around in circles, and balls will be flying everywhere except to the designated catcher. You will not have a shortage of girls who want to be catcher either, especially when they see all the cool gear they get to wear. Of course the number of your volunteers may dwindle when the heat starts to build up under all that gear. The pitcher and catcher are by far the most demanding and critical positions in the game. Teaching these skills to new players can be one of your most time-consuming tasks.

If your league relies solely on coach pitch or a pitching machine, then you can relax a little, but you shouldn't forgo teaching pitching altogether. Your players still need to learn about pitching because eventually they'll be in leagues that do use player pitch. Some youth leagues use player pitch or a combination of coach and player pitch, so you may need to develop a few pitchers for your team this season. Fortunately, most youth leagues do not allow players to pitch a full game until they reach the 10U competitive level. This reduces the pressure on you and the girls, especially if it turns out that you don't have a miniature Cat Osterman on your team.

Pitching Fundamentals

Even to the trained eye of the best pitching instructor in the world, picking the star pitcher out of a group of 6-year-old girls would prove to be difficult. To start out, you should have all the girls try to pitch. For some, pitching will come more naturally than for others. At the beginning of the season, if you think a certain player would be a good pitcher but she does not want to pitch, do not make her. She may develop an interest in pitching halfway through the season, and she may end up being the best pitcher on the team. But if she is being forced to pitch, she will not learn anything—and more important, she will not have any fun. It is not uncommon for players who start pitching when they are 12 years old (or older) to go on to be very good pitchers. Youth softball is all about providing opportunities, and you should not discourage any player from playing a position that she is willing to work at. However, some players will stand out as up-and-coming pitchers. Giving these players more time on the mound will encourage them to continue pitching.

As pitchers advance, coaches will look at two things: power (or speed) and accuracy. Rarely can both be obtained if the fundamental mechanics are not correct. The younger your players, the less you should talk about accuracy or power. Instead, make sure they have the correct motion, and tell them not to worry about where the ball goes. When they aim, they lose power. When they try to throw hard, they lose accuracy. Just as in batting, power and accuracy will come as the mechanics get better. And as with batting, pitching involves lower body mechanics and upper body mechanics. Getting both of them to work together is the tough part.

Pitching is one of the most complex motor skills that you can ask a youngster to perform. Think about it. Starting out facing the batter, the pitcher must stride out toward the batter, turn her body sideways, and time the arm circle just right so the ball hits a spot 17 inches wide and 30 inches tall that is 35 feet away from the pitcher. These are pretty high expectations for a six-year-old. We get excited if our pitchers can throw the ball so that the catcher can catch it while still in a squatted position. For any pitcher, becoming accurate and consistent in throwing the ball will take time and practice. To teach your young pitchers, you must help them learn the five basic steps in the pitching routine: the approach to the pitching rubber and the presentation, the loading phase, the stride, the arm circle and release, and the finish.

The components of pitching are presented in this chapter in the order that they are performed. However, the best way to teach the pitching motion is to teach the components in reverse order. For example, pitchers will find it easier to learn the stride after they have mastered the arm circle. The pitching drills at the end of the chapter can be run individually, but you can create a pitching progression using drills 3, 4, 5, 2, and 6. Performing these drills in this sequence will help players build muscle memory for the pitching motion.

Approach to the Rubber and Presentation

After a pitch, young pitchers often hurry back to the rubber and stand on it, waiting for the next batter. However, the proper approach to the rubber is from behind it, not from the front. Just as there is a setup routine in batting, there is also one for pitching. The following routine can help a pitcher abide by the pitching rules, give her some time to collect herself before the next pitch, and allow her to approach the rubber and present the ball properly:

1. The pitcher receives the ball from the catcher in front of the mound but in the pitching circle.
2. The pitcher walks to the back of the circle (behind the rubber). This is a good time for the pitcher to remind herself how many outs there are and whether any runners are on base.
3. The pitcher walks back up toward the rubber. She stops one step before the rubber and waits until the batter gets into the box. At this point, the rules state that pitcher's hands must be apart. The ball can be in the glove hand or the throwing hand.
4. The pitcher makes her actual approach to the rubber. The pitcher steps onto the rubber (the hands must still be apart) with her stride leg first (the left foot for a right-handed thrower) followed by the drive leg. The toe of the stride leg should touch the back of the rubber, and the heel of the drive leg should touch the front of the rubber (see figure 6.1). The feet should be approximately 1 foot (30 cm) apart. According to ASA and NSA rules, both feet must be in contact with the rubber until the stride leg goes forward.
5. The pitcher brings her hands together above the waist but below the chest. At the same time, she places most of her weight on the

Figure 6.1 Correct position for the pitcher's approach to the rubber.

drive leg and lifts the heel of the stride foot but keeping the toe in contact with the rubber. This movement is known as the presentation because it communicates to the batter that she is preparing to pitch the ball. From this position, the pitcher can focus on her target and get the correct grip on the ball while it's in the glove. The rules usually call for the pitcher to pause in this position as if she were taking a sign from the catcher (but at this level the catcher won't be giving any signs).

Loading Phase

The loading phase, also known as lean and load, is simply rocking back and rocking forward before striding out toward the batter. The loading phase is where most young pitchers develop their individual style, and many try to emulate their favorite college athlete. Nearly all elite pitchers have very similar mechanics once they have loaded their drive leg. Therefore, you can let your players have some fun here, as long as their style adheres to the rules and to good mechanics.

To complete the loading phase, the pitcher raises her hands above her chest and leans back (see figure 6.2). The back heel goes down to the ground as the weight shifts from the driving leg to the striding leg. Then, the pitcher rocks forward and loads her drive leg by lowering her hands to her waist and moving them off to the throwing side while keeping her shoulders square to the batter (figure 6.3). On the rock forward, the pitcher's weight transfers to her front leg, and the front leg bends. Her body position should resemble a sprinter in the starting blocks.

Figure 6.2   During the first part of the loading phase, the pitcher raises her hands and shifts her weight to the stride foot.

Figure 6.3   During the second part of the loading phase, the pitcher shifts her weight back to the drive leg and lowers her hands.

Although the rules allow the pitcher's hands to come apart or stay together at this point, have your pitchers keep their hands together throughout the entire loading phase. Also have them keep their throwing hand in the glove with the ball until they stride forward. Most pitchers separate their hands as they swing the arms down and start to rock forward, but keeping the hands together keeps the technique simple for beginning pitchers. Watch for pitchers who squat down on both legs as they rock forward and do not transfer their weight to the front leg. This is a common mistake for youth pitchers.

Stride

The stride out toward the batter is what attracts most young players to pitching. Because so many things have to happen correctly during the stride, this is also the part of the pitching motion where most things go wrong. With beginning pitchers, focus on one thing: Make sure they get into the K position as the stride foot lands on the ground (see figure 6.4). The K position is almost identical to the scarecrow position for overhand throwing. Striding off the mound is similar to striding forward in the overhand throw except the arm goes in a circle over the shoulder and is released under the shoulder (instead of over the shoulder). In the K position, all the major joints in the body will be on the power line, including the feet, knees, hips, shoulders, and elbows. The hips may be from 45 degrees open to completely open (90 degrees from where they started). The pitcher will be facing third base if she is right handed and first base if she is left handed.

To help pitchers adopt the proper K position, you may need to review the concept of the power line, or line of force, as it relates to pitching. Similar to the power line in throwing (the imaginary line between the thrower and receiver), the power line in pitching is an imaginary line from the pitcher's drive foot to the catcher. Draw a line from the toe of the pitcher's drive foot to the target. When a pitcher is in the K position, both of her feet should be on the power line.

Figure 6.4 During the stride, the pitcher must reach the K position, which requires the full body to be on the line of power.

The easiest way to teach the stride is to break it down into two parts: leg movements and the arm circle. Teach the two parts separately at first. After players have some competence in each, you can put the two together. For now, let's focus on the legs. As the pitcher strides forward with the stride leg, the foot of the drive leg should move over the toe for maximum weight transfer from the rear leg to the front leg. Moving over the toe means that the foot moves over the toe just as it does when the person walks or runs. The person does not turn the foot sideways, and the heel lifts straight up.

When the stride foot lands, the pitcher should touch down on the ball of her foot first and then plant the heel. The toe of the stride foot should be on the power line, and the toes should be pointed in at a 45-degree angle. To help pitchers master this concept, you can use the face of a clock as a reference. If you draw a circle around the foot when it lands, the power line (which is pointed to the target) is 12 o'clock, and the position where the drive foot started is 6 o'clock. For a right-handed pitcher, the stride foot should land on the power line and should be pointed to 1 or 2 o'clock. (For a left-handed pitcher, the toes should point to 10 or 11 o'clock.) If the angle of front foot is too great (toe pointing at 3 o'clock), it prevents the hips from closing at the finish and prevents the drive leg from fully pushing off the power line. If the front foot is straight (12 o'clock), the hips may never open at all, and the throwing arm will go around the throwing side hip to throw the ball, causing the ball to go off to the right for right-handed pitchers and to the left for left-handed pitchers.

Some coaches teach their pitchers to pivot the drive foot 45 degrees out before striding forward. Pivoting can assist in opening the hips, but the motion is not as efficient for pushing forward. Other coaches teach their pitchers that the hips need to open completely during the stride. Try not to get too technical about the hips with beginning pitchers. How far their hips need to get open will vary because their bodies vary. The hips will take care of themselves as the players get the timing down between their stride leg and their arm circle. Now, let's take a look at the arms.

Arm Circle and Release

Your pitchers will need lots of reps to work on developing a consistent release point. This is the most difficult part of the pitch for young players to master. Balls will be flying over the catcher's head as you begin work— and some will be flying over the backstop! A common sense approach to teaching the release is to build up to the full motion from the release point and to incorporate the stride as soon as possible.

To help your pitchers learn a proper arm circle, break the arm circle down into four quarters. Use the hands of a clock as a metaphor to identify where the arm is placed for each stage of the circle. Looking at a pitcher from the third-base side of the mound, imagine the pitcher's arms as the arms on the face of a clock; the pitching arm moves counterclockwise starting next to the leg or hip (6 o'clock). For the first quarter of the circle, the ball and hand travel directly out in front (3 o'clock). For the second quarter, the ball and hand continue to move counterclockwise to a position directly above the head (12 o'clock). During the third quarter the arm travels to a position in which the elbow is pointing down (about 10 o'clock or 9 o'clock). When the pitching arm is in the third quarter, the glove hand should point straight to the catcher. As the arm starts to move down the backside of the circle, it accelerates and the elbow leads the ball. The final quarter of the arm circle is the movement from the K position to the release point. The release should happen between the 6 o'clock and 7 o'clock positions. At first, many young pitchers will make the mistake of releasing the ball out in front of the body and above the waist.

As the arms separate and move into the K position (quarter 3), the shoulders should open, and the front and rear elbows should both naturally get in line with the target. The throwing elbow should be slightly bent when the pitcher gets to the K position. The palm of the throwing hand should be facing out to the side as if the player were holding a glass of water. If the palm is facing down, the wrist will load too early, causing the throwing arm to lock out straight behind the pitcher. If the palm is up while coming down the back end of the circle, the wrist will not load in time, and the pitcher will lose velocity.

The pitcher will throw the ball underhand by accelerating her elbow to the 6 o'clock position, which causes a whipping action. The elbow will actually decelerate when it gets to the 6 o'clock position, allowing the ball and hand to pass in front of the elbow before the elbow continues forward in the follow-through. But the elbow and wrist snap together. The shoulders should remain open and in line with the target until the ball is released. The longer the shoulders remain open, or in line with the target, the more accurate the pitch will be.

The glove hand should be coming down with the throwing hand, but a split second after the throwing arm goes down. The pitcher's posture should be upright and slightly back at the release point. If the pitcher is leaning forward at release, she will lose speed and accuracy because the arm will not whip at the bottom of the circle. In other words, the nose should never be in front of the belly button when the ball is being released. The arm should be loose after release; the hand should follow the ball to the target, and the elbow should be extended away from the body and pointed forward toward the catcher.

To combine the arm circle with the stride, have your pitchers focus on starting the first quarter of the arm circle just as they stride forward. They should pick up their stride knee just as the glove and ball move in front of them and start to move up. A key point is that the speed of the arm circle does not dictate how fast the pitcher will throw. The speed of the arm circle is dictated by the stride. The shorter and quicker the stride, the faster the arm circle needs to be. The longer and slower the stride, the slower the arm circle needs to be. Speed and power are determined by the acceleration of the arm in the last quarter and how much momentum is generated by the legs as they stride and drive forward.

Finish

The pitcher should finish the pitch in an upright and balanced position, facing the batter with both hands out in front and ready to field the ball (see figure 6.5). This may seem simple, but you'll be amazed to see how many pitchers fall over, spin, trip, stop abruptly, or lean one way or the other. That being said, you do not need to spend much time emphasizing the correct finish. As long as you have taught the pitchers the proper arm circle, and then incorporated the proper footwork, the finish will look natural, and the pitchers will finish in a good defensive position. The finish is a result of the previous movements. If the pitchers are not finishing in a good defensive position, chances are their footwork is incorrect or the timing of the arm circle with their footwork is off.

Figure 6.5 In the finish position, the pitcher should be ready to field the ball.

Mental Preparation

In addition to teaching the physical mechanics of pitching, you need to prepare your pitchers mentally before they will be ready to take the mound at game time. Make sure your pitchers understand the rules for your particular league. In many youth leagues, pitchers are not allowed to walk any batters. After four balls, a coach pitches until the batter puts a ball into play. The pitcher can, however, strike out a batter if she does not pitch four balls first. Because of this rule, some coaches offer the following advice to their beginning pitchers: "Just throw strikes; let your defense help you out."

If you have an Olympic-caliber defense, this is good advice, but in youth softball most games are lost by bad throws and catches. Additionally, if your pitchers go on to play at more competitive levels, they'll face

Pitching Quick Start Cadence

Teaching the pitching motion in segments is undoubtedly the best way to make sure your players learn the proper technique. However, many young players lack patience, and they may start emulating what they saw when they watched an older sister or someone else pitching. If any of your pitchers lack the patience to learn pitching using the progression, you can use a cadence (*one-two-three-four-shut the door-finish*) that lets them pitch using the full motion. This cadence is fully described in drill 1 on page 132. Be warned, this method will result in a lot of wild pitches at first. This is a good time to use backstops and lots of balls and give the catcher a break. You can use this cadence even if you are teaching the progression. The cadence helps get rid of some of the girls' jitters and lets them have a little fun.

better hitters, and throwing it across the plate will not be good advice. Players need to understand the fundamentals of softball from the first day they step onto the field. For a pitcher, the most fundamental mental aspect of the game is to get the out. The pitcher does this either by striking out the batter or by putting the ball in a spot where the batter will not be able to hit the ball hard.

Although the ultimate goal is for pitchers to get the out, you, of course, are working with beginners and you have to remember that being on the mound is intimidating for a young pitcher. Therefore, the number one rule for coaching your young pitchers is to keep it positive and keep encouraging them. Make sure the feedback your pitchers hear from you and the parents is not overwhelming. Some young players with natural ability refuse to pitch because in the past they were never "good enough" either for their coach or parents. Try not to focus on mechanics during a game; instead, focus on effort and composure. No matter how badly it may be going that day, the pitcher should always look as if she is winning the game 10 to 0. Pitching is demanding and takes hard work and practice. If young pitchers are willing to work hard at practice, all they will need to be successful is for someone to believe in them—and you get to be that someone.

Catching Fundamentals

Although the rules for pitching will vary by league, most leagues do allow catchers. Of course, 6- or 7-year-old catchers will usually not catch a lot of the pitched balls coming at them; however, dressed in all their armor, they will at least look like a catcher. To keep games moving, a coach or parent may be positioned behind the catcher during the game. This

Figure 6.6 Proper setup position for a catcher.

coach can stop the balls that get by the young catcher and can make sure that the catcher is set up correctly for each pitch. Like selecting pitchers, a good practice is to let everyone try on the gear and receive some balls. Some girls will like it immediately, and others will let you know that they don't want to catch.

At the first practice, make sure you explain all the catcher's equipment and how to put it on. To help the players learn, you can time them on how fast they can put on and take off the equipment. You also need to teach them the correct setup position. The catcher can move forward and back in the catcher's box to adjust for how the batter sets up in the batter's box. The catcher's feet cannot go in front of the rear chalk line of the batter's box until the ball has been pitched. When squatted down, the catcher must feel comfortable and must remain on the balls of her feet to be able to stand up quickly. The catcher's feet should be slightly wider than the shoulders, with the glove-side foot just slightly in front of the throwing-side foot (see figure 6.6). This will set the catcher up for a good powerful throw. Make sure the catcher does not sit straight up or lean forward too far. The glove hand is in front of the body, the arm is extended; and the elbow should be out to the side, not below the glove (which is a common mistake for youth catchers). The throwing hand is behind the catcher's back or grabbing her leg. This keeps the hand from getting hit by a foul tip or missed ball.

Practicing the catcher's position is essential because the catchers will need to be prepared to be close to the batter during games. At higher levels of play, the catcher will have to know a great deal about strategy. As a youth coach, you will not be able to teach the catchers everything they need to know, but you should ensure that your catchers learn three fundamental skills: catching the ball, blocking the ball, and throwing the ball quickly with power and accuracy.

Catching

The rules for catching pitched balls are similar to the rules for catching other types of thrown balls. The catcher will want to receive the ball with her fingers up. However, for catchers, the point of reference for whether their fingers should be up or down is not the waist (which should be at roughly the same level as the knees when the catcher is in the squatted position) but rather the knees. So, if the ball is above the catcher's knees, the fingers should be pointed up; if the ball is caught below the knees, then the fingers should be pointed down.

Catchers should make the catch out in front of them with a flexed front arm. Most beginners have a tendency to let their glove move back when they catch the ball. Try teaching your catchers early on to push the glove forward as they catch the ball (see figure 6.7). This helps the umpire determine the location of the pitch. If the catcher allows the glove to come back, as if she is absorbing the throw, this does not give the umpire a good look at where the pitch was thrown.

Figure 6.7 Catchers should push forward when catching the ball to make sure the catch is made in front of the body.

When teaching young catchers to catch the ball, start out using Wiffle, tennis, or sponge balls. Have the catcher assume a full squatted position without a glove. This way the player can see that her fingers are pointed up and that her palm is facing forward and away from her when catching the ball. Many beginning players will hold their hands correctly all the way to the point of actually catching the ball; then, at the last second, they will turn their hands so that their fingers are pointed down to the ground and their palms are facing up (as if they did not want the ball to hit the ground). If your catchers have this problem, you can try the following: Stand next to the catcher, and instead of throwing the ball to her, simply move the ball in the air with your hand and place it in the catcher's hand while her hand is still in the correct position. Then you can do short throws and slowly move back until the catcher has the hang of it.

Blocking

For balls that travel below the knees, not only will the catcher need to turn her hand so the fingers are facing down, she will also need to position her body to block the ball and prevent it from getting by her. Many catchers will try to field the ball instead of blocking the ball. As catchers get older, some may be able to pull balls out of the dirt without getting into a

Figure 6.8   Correct position for a catcher to block a ball.

blocking position, but this is very rare and not advisable. The blocking position for a catcher is having both knees on the ground and putting the glove between the knees (with no space between the glove and either leg); the tip of the glove should be in the dirt (see figure 6.8). The upper body will be upright with a slight curve in the middle to cup the ball in case it bounces up. The catcher's head should be tilted down with the chin on the chest. The biggest challenge for youth catchers is that they will want to catch the ball when blocking. Instruct them to deflect the ball to a spot in front of them, preferably home plate; by doing so they have a better chance to keep base runners from advancing to the next base on a wild pitch. At the youth level, catchers are likely to see a lot of wild pitches.

The first rule for blocking is that the catcher needs to center her body in the path of the ball. If the ball is coming straight at the catcher but going low in the dirt, all the catcher needs to do is kick her feet back and drop to her knees in front of the ball. If the ball is going to the left, then the catcher needs to push off her right foot to move left and drop to her knees in front of the ball. The technique will be the exact opposite if the ball is going to the catcher's right. For young catchers, you may consider it a success if they drop to their knees at all. The shin guards are mostly for protecting the catcher's shins from the ground and foul tips, not from low-pitched balls.

Throwing

The third essential skill for a catcher is being able to throw the ball quickly with power and accuracy. The most critical factor in getting rid of the ball quickly is how long it takes for the catcher to transfer the ball from the glove to her throwing hand. This is referred to as transfer time. The throwing mechanics of "secure, separate, and snap" (see chapter 4) apply to the catcher as well. Catchers need to secure the ball as they start to move into the throwing position. The ball should be fully separated from the glove before the catcher gets to a full upright standing position. The transfer should happen in front of the body near the throwing shoulder;

the palm of the throwing hand should be facing up, and the palm of the glove hand should be facing down. This ensures that the throwing elbow is positioned to go up and above the shoulder on the overhand throw.

The footwork of the catcher determines the power and accuracy of the throw. Catchers may use any of three methods. In the first method, the catcher pops up into a throwing position. In the second method, the catcher rotates on her throwing foot so that she is sideways to her target. In the third method, the catcher incorporates a step and throw. For beginning catchers, the step-and-throw method is a good option because it is consistent with the footwork used by fielders when throwing the ball. This method is a condensed version of the three steps used in basic throwing. The catcher is already set up with her glove-side foot slightly in front of her throwing foot. For this reason, she needs to take only two steps to complete the throw. After the catcher has caught the ball, she brings it to her throwing shoulder as she starts to move into an upright position. As the catcher is securing the ball (while still in a semi-crouched position), she steps forward with her throwing foot and plants the foot with the toes facing out (see figure 6.9). Once the ball is secured with her throwing hand, she separates the ball as she is taking her second step toward the target; this step is taken with the glove-side foot (see figure 6.10). She then pushes off with her rear leg and snaps the ball to the target, which will usually be the pitcher.

Figure 6.9   As the catcher plants her throwing-side foot, she begins to come out of her squatted position.

Figure 6.10   The catcher separates the ball and steps with the glove-side foot just before snapping the ball to the target.

Drill 1 Quick Start Cadence

EQUIPMENT   A throw-down pitching rubber and ball for each pitcher

PURPOSE   This drill lets beginning pitchers pitch using full motion. It can be used as a substitute for or in addition to the standard pitching progression.

PROCEDURE   Have your pitchers line up along the third-base line, facing the fence. Give each pitcher a ball. Place a pitching rubber in front of each player (or draw a makeshift rubber in the dirt); the player should stand 5 feet (152 cm) behind the rubber. Have each player use her foot to draw a straight line from the center of the rubber to the fence. On your command, the pitcher's make the usual approach. You call out the pitching cadence and have the pitchers pause for one second at each phase:

- *One*. The pitcher presents the ball (as with the usual pitching pro-gression).
- *Two*. The pitcher shifts her weight from the drive foot to the stride foot.
- *Three*. The pitcher shifts her weight back to the drive foot.
- *Four*. The pitcher reaches the K position in the stride.
- *Shut the door*. The pitcher releases the ball at the end of the arm circle.
- *Finish*. Pitcher ends in an upright and balanced position.

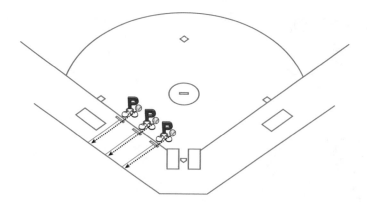

COACHING POINTS   For first-time pitchers, do the drill without a ball, and add the ball only when the players are able to successfully demon-strate the movements. At the "shut the door" command (the release), the pitchers should focus on whipping the ball to the fence.

Drill 2 Loading

BEGINNER

EQUIPMENT One ball to start; a catcher or backstop once the initial 10 to 15 reps are completed

PURPOSE This drill helps pitchers learn the proper footwork for both the stride leg and the drive leg.

PROCEDURE The pitcher is positioned on the mound without a ball. Place a softball on the ground just inside of the pitcher's drive foot. The pitcher shifts her weight forward to her drive leg, bending at the hips, knees, and ankles until she feels as if she is going to fall forward (see photo). The pitcher pushes off her drive foot as she is striding forward, pushes her arms out hard to the first quarter of the arm circle, and completes the pitching motion. The goal is to make sure the ball does not move during the entire pitching motion. Complete 10 reps.

COACHING POINTS Without the ball in her hands, the pitcher can focus on just her footwork. Any time a pitcher is struggling with her footwork, take the ball out of her hands and have her simulate pitching. This will allow her to focus on what her feet are doing, and she will not need to be concerned about where the ball is going. Make sure the pitcher still goes through the full throwing motion and finishes the pitch.

MODIFICATIONS When the pitcher can complete 10 good reps in which the ball doesn't move, have her continue the drill by pitching a ball to a catcher. For a pitching progression and warm-ups, this is the fourth drill that the players should perform (after drill 5).

Drill 3 Kneeling K

EQUIPMENT   Bucket of balls; catcher or backstop for each pitcher; pads for pitchers to kneel on

PURPOSE   This drill helps pitchers learn the proper release point and the whip of the arm at release.

PROCEDURE   Pitchers are kneeling on one knee about 15 feet (4.5 m) from the catcher. The knee of the pitcher's drive leg is on the ground; the foot of the stride leg is on the ground to the front (with the knee up). The knee and the foot are on the power line, and the pitcher's hips and front foot are at a 45-degree angle. Pitchers start with both arms hanging straight down in front of them with the ball in the glove. At the command of "Up!" the pitcher gets into the K position by separating her hands (see photo): The throwing arm moves back and up, and the glove hand moves forward and up. At the command of "Down!" the pitcher accelerates her throwing arm to her side and pitches the ball.

COACHING POINTS   Make sure that the pitcher's throwing wrist is in the correct position when she is in the K position and that the elbow is slightly bent (approximately a 45-degree angle). If a player has problems holding the ball correctly while in the K position, place a cup of water in her hand so she has to turn her hand sideways. This will enable her to see the correct position. The players should be leaning back as they release the ball. If needed, give them verbal cues, telling them to keep their nose behind their belly button. Make sure that their shoulders don't overrotate when getting into the K position or when throwing the ball. The elbow must decelerate when it reaches the hip; however, make sure the players do not artificially stop their elbow when pitching the ball. The players should finish with a loose arm after the ball has been released.

MODIFICATIONS   When the players are becoming competent at the drill, which usually takes 20 to 30 reps, they can do the drill without commands. To use this drill in a pitching progression for practice or warm-up, start the drill with the pitchers throwing from 15 feet for 10 reps, move them back to 20 to 25 feet (6.1 to 7.6 m) for another 10 reps, and then move them back to 25 to 35 feet (7.6 to 10.6 m) for the last 10 reps.

Drill 4 Arm Circles

EQUIPMENT   Bucket of balls; catcher or backstop for each pitcher; pads for the pitchers to kneel on

PURPOSE   This drill teaches players the pitching arm circle by isolating the upper body movements of the pitching motion.

PROCEDURE   Pitchers are kneeling on one knee about 15 feet (4.5 m) from the catcher. The knee of the pitcher's drive leg is on the ground; the foot of the stride leg is on the ground to the front (with the knee up). The knee and the foot are on the power line, and the pitcher's hips and front foot are at a 45-degree angle. Pitchers start with both arms hanging straight down in front of them and the ball in the glove. You will give the players a count of four. When you call out "One," the pitchers start the arm circle and pause at the first quarter. When you call out "Two," the pitchers continue the arm circle to the second quarter and then pause (see photo). When you call out "Three," the pitchers continue the arm circle to the third quarter (or the K position) and then pause. When you call out "Four," the pitchers pitch the ball by accelerating their arm down to the release point. After 10 to 20 reps with commands, the pitchers can complete reps on their own count without pausing in any of the positions.

COACHING POINTS   When the players are doing arm circles, make sure that their glove hand goes up and in front of them as they start the arm circle. Players often make two common errors when doing this drill. The first is releasing the ball too late. If players repeatedly hold onto the ball too long and release it out in front and above the waist, have them skip the ball to the target. Make sure the players throw the ball hard when doing this drill. The second error is that players will stop their throwing arm at release, or the throwing arm will be too tight after the player has thrown the ball. To help players work on making sure their arm follows through in a loose and relaxed manner, position the players an arm's length away from a backstop with a loose net. Have the players throw into the net. After they have released the ball, they must try to grab the net with their throwing hand. We call this "chasing the ball."

MODIFICATIONS   If you are using the drill in a pitching progression or a warm-up, this should be the second drill the players perform (after drill 3), and you should gradually increase the throwing distance (players throw from 15 feet for 10 reps, move back to 20 to 25 feet for another 10 reps, then move back to 25 to 35 feet for the last 10 reps).

Drill 5 Standing Circles

EQUIPMENT   Bucket of balls; catcher or backstop for each pitcher

PURPOSE   This drill helps pitchers learn the proper timing of the arm circle with the landing of the stride foot.

PROCEDURE   Pitchers stand sideways about 20 feet (6.1 m) from the catcher. The pitcher is facing slightly toward the catcher with her glove-side shoulder pointing to the target. The pitcher's feet are approximately shoulder-width apart, the toes are on the power line at a 45-degree angle, and the stride foot is closest to the catcher. The hands are together near the belly button with the throwing hand gripping the ball in the glove at the start of each pitch. As the pitcher performs the arm circle, the front foot should lift up and toward the catcher at the beginning of the arm circle, and start going down when the throwing arm is at the peak of the circle (see photo). The foot should be planted when the arm is three quarters of the way through the circle or all the way closed to the target. The pitcher throws 10 to 15 reps from 20 feet, then moves back to 25 feet (7.6 m) for 10 reps, and then back to 30 feet (9.1 m) for 10 reps.

COACHING POINTS   The main point of focus is that the front knee goes up with the arms as they go to the first-quarter position of the arm circle and the leg comes back down to plant as the throwing arm continues to the second quarter of the circle. The ball should be separated from the glove after both hands have passed the first quarter (at or above the shoulders); the pitcher should keep the glove hand pointed at the target. As the pitcher continues with the arm circle, make sure that the biceps of the throwing hand passes by the ear. The arm should reach the third quarter when the front foot has landed back on the power line. The stride foot should land at a 45-degree angle, and the pitcher should finish with the hips at least 45 degrees to the target.

MODIFICATIONS   As the pitchers get the timing down (with their front leg landing when the arm circle is at the third quarter), have them start pushing forward with their drive leg as they start the arm circle and lift their stride leg. The knee of the drive leg should be moving toward the stride leg as the ball is being released. If you are using the drill in a pitching progression or a warm-up, this should be the third drill the players perform (after drill 4).

Drill 6 Walk-Through

🥎🥎 INTERMEDIATE

EQUIPMENT Bucket of balls; catcher or backstop for each pitcher; throw-down or makeshift (drawn in the dirt) rubber for each pitcher

PURPOSE This drill helps pitchers incorporate lower body drive and increase forward momentum.

PROCEDURE The pitcher has a ball, and the catcher is positioned 30 to 40 feet (9.1 to 12.2 m) away. The pitcher starts out three steps behind the pitching rubber. When ready, the pitcher takes three steps, starting with the drive foot. On the third step, the drive foot plants on the front edge of the rubber, and the pitcher pitches the ball to the catcher. Complete 10 to 20 reps.

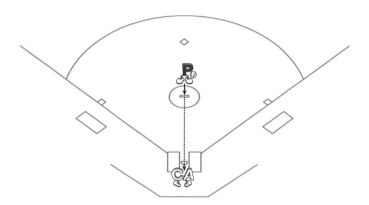

COACHING POINTS The main focus of this drill is to get the pitchers to become more dynamic off the mound in order to create as much forward momentum as they can muster. This will be tricky for some youngsters because they will not know how to swing their arms while trying to get into a good loaded position. When the drive foot plants on the rubber, the pitcher must get all her weight to the drive leg, and she must lift the knee of her stride leg up and toward the catcher. Don't worry about mechanics as the pitchers are trying to get their timing down.

MODIFICATIONS Once the players have demonstrated that they can do this drill with some consistency, you can incorporate long toss. To do this, have the pitchers complete 10 reps from the mound and then continue to take two or three steps farther back until they cannot reach the catcher anymore. When doing long toss, players are allowed to throw the ball with an arc in the pitch. This is a good drill for helping pitchers make sure that the arm stays long and loose during the pitch.

Drill 7 One Up, One Down

EQUIPMENT   Bucket of balls

PURPOSE   This drill teaches pitchers to hit spots, and it helps catchers learn the strike zone.

PROCEDURE   Assign a pitcher and catcher to their respective positions on the field. (If a catcher isn't available, you or another coach can catch the balls.) The catcher provides a target with her glove in one of the four corners of the strike zone (see photo). The pitcher must hit that spot without forcing the catcher to move her glove. The pitcher starts with 5 points. If the pitcher hits her spot, she goes "one up," and if she misses her spot, she goes "one down." If she gets to zero, she loses; if she gets to 10, she wins.

COACHING POINTS   If the catcher moves her glove within reason, you may still consider the pitch to be good. If the catcher has to move her glove to another corner, the pitch should not be considered good.

MODIFICATIONS   For beginning pitchers, modify the scoring system. For every spot the pitcher hits, she goes two up; for every spot she misses, she goes one down. As the pitchers get more accurate, you can go back to one up and one down.

Drill 8 Tennis Ball Catch

EQUIPMENT   Bucket of tennis balls (20 to 30 balls)

PURPOSE   This drill teaches catchers to squeeze their glove when catching balls.

PROCEDURE   The catcher sets up behind the plate with all her gear on except her glove. The coach stands about 10 feet (3 m) in front of the catcher and tosses tennis balls underhand to her. The catcher can only use one hand to catch the ball. Of course, the coach is not whipping the ball in there, but the path of the ball should be flat. Once the player has done 10 to 30 reps and is consistently squeezing the ball, she should put a glove on. The coach then throws the balls a bit harder for another 10 to 30 reps.

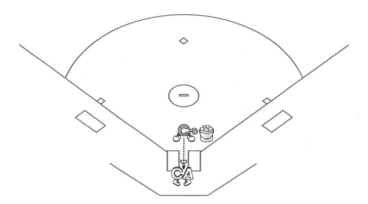

COACHING POINTS   Tennis balls have a tendency to pop out of the glove, so the catcher will have to make sure she squeezes the glove tightly to catch each ball.

Drill 9 Block 10-10-10

🎾🎾 INTERMEDIATE

EQUIPMENT   Bucket of tennis balls (30 balls)

PURPOSE   This drill teaches catchers to block balls.

PROCEDURE   Draw a half oval around the front of home plate, starting from the back corner of one batter's box and extending to the back corner of the other batter's box. The catcher sets up behind the plate. Skip tennis balls to the catcher from 20 to 25 feet (6.1 to 7.6 m) in front of the catcher. The balls should bounce somewhere near home plate and up into the catcher. The catcher has to use her equipment to block the ball. The goal for the catcher is to block the ball and get each ball to end up inside of the half oval. This means the catcher will have to adjust her body to make sure the ball bounces back into the half oval. Skip 10 balls down the middle, the next 10 to the right, and another 10 to the left.

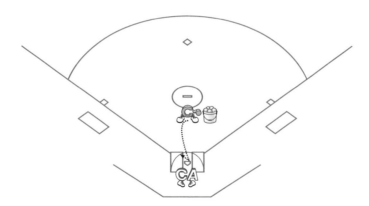

COACHING POINTS   The catcher will need to move her feet and turn her body toward home plate if she is to deflect the balls back into the circle. This teaches the catcher to keep the ball in front of her.

MODIFICATIONS   If you have more than one catcher, you can have them compete to see who can block the most balls back into the half oval.

Drill 10 Quick Throw Down

EQUIPMENT   Bucket of balls; stopwatch

PURPOSE   This drill teaches catchers to transfer the ball correctly and throw quickly.

PROCEDURE   For this drill, you need a pitcher, a catcher, and a shortstop in their respective positions on the field. The pitcher pitches a ball to the catcher, who catches it using the proper technique and then throws the ball to second base. The shortstop should start in her defensive position and should yell, "Going!" after the pitcher releases the ball. This is to inform the catcher that the base runner on first is stealing second. Time the catcher from the point when the pitched ball hits her glove until the ball hits the shortstop's glove at second base. A good time for young players is a time under four seconds. Limit the amount of reps to 15 throws per catcher per session.

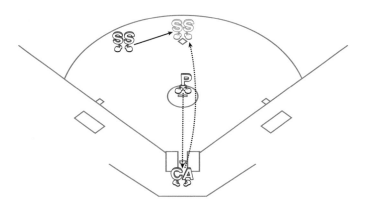

COACHING POINTS   Watch to make sure the catcher transfers the ball to her throwing hand before standing up. Remember that not many players under eight years old will be able to throw from home to second without bouncing the ball a few times.

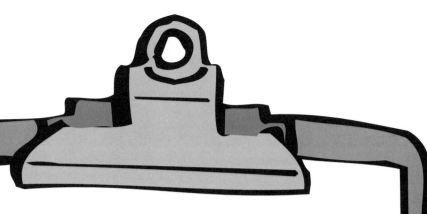

The Coach's Clipboard

✔ The pitching routine includes five basic steps: the approach to the rubber and the presentation, the loading phase, the stride, the arm circle and release, and the finish.

✔ A young pitcher must master the correct body mechanics of pitching in order to throw with power or accuracy.

✔ To illustrate the power line, draw a line in the dirt that extends from the toe of the pitcher's drive foot to the catcher.

✔ The most critical body position a pitcher must assume is the K position.

✔ Keep beginning pitchers motivated in practice and games by focusing on the positives.

✔ Make sure that the catcher's gear fits correctly and comfortably.

✔ Beginning catchers need to make sure they can catch the ball correctly, block the ball, and throw the ball with speed and accuracy.

✔ To throw with speed and accuracy, catchers need to use their legs and incorporate a two-step throw.

On-Field Execution

Your expectations for your team's on-the-field execution will depend on the age of your players. You may be satisfied if you can keep your fielders from doing cartwheels while the pitch is being delivered. Or you may be disappointed if the fielders are not focusing on the batter and expecting the ball. Either way, you need to accept that you will not have enough time during practice to cover all of the possible offensive and defensive situations your players may face. Most of their learning about these situations will come from playing the games. This is not to say that you shouldn't work on defensive and offensive situational strategies. However, you should limit the time you spend on them because this type of practice often requires the coach to focus on only a few players at a time. This leads to a lot of standing around for the players you're not working with. And that's one sure way to encourage those players to start writing their names in the dirt.

Offensive Strategy

A simple and effective offensive plan can consist of having a good at-bat and running hard and smart. There will be times, Coach, when you just want to go to a corner of the dugout, roll up in a fetal position, and pray that the game will end soon. Other times you will beam with pride when the girls put the ball into play and run aggressively to each base, making you look like a genius. The simpler you can make your offensive strategy, the more success you will have.

Batting Strategy

A good at-bat is determined by how many pitches the batter sees and whether the batter makes solid contact with the ball. Notice that this description does not include "getting a hit" or "getting on base." That's because in the game of softball, a batter can fail 7 out of 10 times (.300 batting average) and still be considered very successful. Players need to understand that they may only get 1 or 2 at-bats during a game. If they swing at the first three pitches in each at-bat, they may only see six pitches total for the game. Some young players swing at anything and everything. Players who take this approach to batting may see only two pitches during the whole game. A better approach would be for each player to try to see five or more pitches per at-bat.

You can only do so much in practice to teach players how to swing properly (i.e., swing level through the zone). Once game time arrives, the instruction is over, and you need to focus on what you can do to help them be successful and make solid contact with the ball. Typically, players have one of three types of swings: a level swing, an uppercut swing, or a chopping swing (the bat goes from high to low through the strike zone, as if the player is chopping down a tree with an ax). For the few batters with level swings, their pitch is a belt-high pitch that comes down the middle of the plate. For batters with an uppercut swing, their pitch is low and outside. And for batters with chopping swings, their pitch is usually high and inside.

Once you have identified how each player swings, you can help the players identify *their* pitch during practices. An effective way to do this is to front toss balls to the batter, trying to place the ball where she can make good contact. Emphasize to the batter that this is her pitch to hit. Come game time, you can reinforce the message by reminding the player to look for her pitch—just like in practice—and to swing only at those pitches. Assure your batters that watching a strike or two go by is acceptable because this is part of the offensive plan.

Outs and Tagging Up

Take time during offensive practices to explain the three ways that batters or runners can be called out without any help from the defense: The player interferes with a fielder who is trying to field a ball, the player is struck by the ball while not on base, and the player improperly leaves a base. The last situation requires a bit more explanation. A player can improperly leave a base in two ways. One way is by failing to tag up on a fly ball. You need to explain tagging up starting at the first practice. You may not expect a seven- or eight-year-old to tag up on all pop-ups;

however, the players must understand that if the ball is caught in the air and the base runners left their base before the catch (i.e., they did not tag up), they can be thrown out at the base they left.

As a general rule, you should tell your players to run on every hit ball. Getting the girls to run right away on a hit ball will take some work. Before taking off, most young players want to be a spectator for a while and watch the ball as it travels past the defensive players. Of course, once you do get the players to run hard and aggressively, they'll inevitably get doubled up. This happens when the batter hits a pop fly and the base runner is already at the next base (without tagging up) when the fielder catches the ball. The defense then throws to the previous base, and your runner is out. When this happens, your player will often think that she has done something wrong; she may look at you through teary eyes and say, "I did what you told me to do, Coach." This is why tagging up is one of the first things you should teach your players.

For runners on first or second base, you should teach the following strategy to get the base runners to run aggressively while also being ready for pop-ups hit to the outfield: The base runners should leave the base immediately, but if the ball is hit in the air, they should advance only to halfway between the bases and then stop (see figure 7.1). They should watch to see if the fielder catches the ball. If the ball is caught, they need to run back to the base they were just at. If the ball is dropped, they can run to the next base. For pop-ups and line drives to the infield, the base runners should freeze where they are and watch to see if the ball clears the infield or drops to the ground before they advance to the next base.

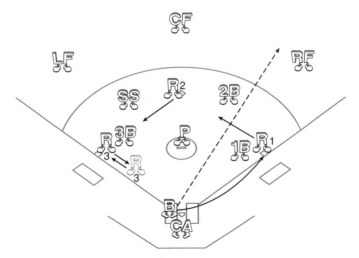

Figure 7.1   On a pop fly, base runners on first and second should run halfway to the next base and watch to see what happens before running on or tagging up. A base runner on third should tag up immediately, wait for the ball to contact the defender, and run home (assuming she can make it safely).

If the runner is on third base, the strategy is a little different. When a pop fly is hit, a runner who has just left third base should run back to third immediately; the runner should stand on the base until the fielder touches the ball (figure 7.1). Once the ball hits any part of the defender, the runner on third can leave the base and run home. It does not matter if the ball bounces straight up out of the fielder's glove and the fielder catches it on the way back down. As long as the runner has gone back to the base and the ball makes contact with a defender, the runner can run home. Although most leagues follow this rule, be sure to check with your league umpires to make sure that this is the ruling they use.

A second way for a player to leave the base improperly is to leave before the pitcher releases the ball. In softball, base runners cannot lead off. The "look back" rule is also unique to softball. This rule prevents a base runner from baiting the pitcher into throwing the ball to try to get her out. The rule applies only when the pitcher has possession of the ball in the pitching circle. At this point, all runners must make an immediate decision to go back to the base that they just came from or advance to the next base. A runner who stands still and waits to see what the pitcher is going to do will be called out.

Defensive Strategy

Your defensive plan should also be very simple. (Remember your audience!) You may hear some coaches say that the defense should always go after the lead runner. However, this philosophy only works well with players who have a thorough knowledge of the game and with a team that has good chemistry and solid communication skills. Few, if any, youth softball teams can play at this level. Besides, at this age, the players don't need to know all the situations they may face when playing. If your team gives up five unearned runs, the odds are pretty good that they'll be able to score some runs of their own in the next inning or two.

Keeping your team's defensive strategy simple will make things easier for you too. When I (Bob) was a novice coach, I sometimes found myself yelling "Where's the play girls?"—not because I wanted to test them to see if they learned anything, but because I wasn't sure either. I didn't know if it would be wise to go after the lead runner or if the players should go for the routine out and let the lead runner score. A defensive plan for a youth softball team may consist of mastering the routine play and communicating. This might sound simplistic, but the goals in this plan can be difficult to accomplish if you do not emphasize them early and throughout the season.

Outs and Force Plays

Even if your league does not record outs, your defense can still work on meeting the defensive objective in the game, which is, of course, to keep the opponent from scoring runs by getting three outs per inning. The defense can get an out on the offense in four basic ways: Three strikes are called on the batter, a fielder catches the hit ball before it touches the ground, a fielder with possession of the ball uses the ball to tag a runner, and a fielder with possession of the ball touches the base before the runner (who is advancing to that base) touches the base.

The first three ways to get an out are fairly simple, but the fourth option depends on whether the situation is a force play. A force play is a play when a runner *must* advance to the next base after the ball is hit. Of course, the play at any base can be a force play if a runner must advance to the base because other runners are occupying the bases behind her. Explain to your players that the play at first base is always a force play because the batter must run to first. Work to help your players perfect the throw to first after fielding the ball so that this play becomes routine. For the first-base player, the simplest way to make the play is to touch the base when or after receiving the throw. She can also tag the runner if the runner is still in front of her when she fields or receives a thrown ball; however, when a defender uses a tag, there is always a chance that the ball will be knocked out of the glove.

Another force-play situation occurs when a runner is off the base when a fly ball is caught, and the runner must tag up. Defenders have the option of throwing the ball to the base to try to get the runner out before she can get back to the base. The defender covering the base can get a force-out on the runner by touching the base before she does. A defender may also use the ball to tag out the runner before she gets back onto the base. With young players, the situation often becomes entertaining when a fielder catches a fly ball and there are runners on base. Coaches and parents from both teams yell a barrage of mixed messages: "Tag her!" "Throw the ball!" "Run!" and "Tag up!" The fielder who catches the ball may simply lock up and stand there not knowing what to do with the ball. Or, thinking that she must stop the runner, the fielder may throw the ball to the base the runner is running to instead of the base the runner needs to tag up on. Luckily, players usually don't consistently hit pop-ups or catch fly balls until the age of 10 or 11. By that time, the players will have a few games and practices under their belts and will be able to make good decisions.

Avoid using phrases such as "Get the easy out." This language may not accurately communicate your desired strategy to your players, and it could be offensive to the opposing team. Although you are probably not calling the batter an "easy out," she may take it that way. There are no easy outs in youth softball, but there are routine outs and routine plays. The term *routine* is not offensive, and it sets an attitude of confidence for your players by reminding them that it's a task they can accomplish easily.

During the first couple of practices (and then frequently throughout the season), you should look for opportunities to stop a play and ask the players where the force play is. This will help you make sure that the players understand the difference between the force play and the nonforce play. Do not take anything for granted. We'll never forget one player's response when she was asked what a force play was: "Well, my dad is forcing me to play softball."

Magnet Principle

The magnet principle is a basic concept that can be used to help young players learn defensive coverage. In this strategy, the players pretend that the ball is a gigantic magnet and that they are all pieces of metal that are attracted to it. Wherever the ball is hit, the defenders need to start moving to it, not to see who can get to it first, but to provide backup and assume supportive roles once the ball is picked up. If a defender comes to a base before she gets to the ball, then her responsibility is to be on the base. Make sure you explain that only one person is allowed to pick up the ball; otherwise, you may have several players tackling each other to get to the ball. At other times, you may see several defenders standing around the ball in what appears to be a board meeting to decide who will pick up the ball.

To begin with, make sure your defenders know where their basic setup position should be on the field (see figure 7.2) when they're preparing for a hit. They can't move to the correct coverage position if they don't start in the correct place. The pitcher starts on the rubber and the catcher starts behind home plate. The first and third base defenders should be approximately 3 feet (9 m) in front of their base and 3 feet from the foul line. The second base defender and shortstop should be about half way between the bases and just behind the base path. The center fielder should be directly behind second base and about 20 to 40 feet (6 to 12 m) from the base. The left fielder plays at about the same depth as the centerfielder and should be half way between the shortstop and third base defender. The right fielder plays at a similar depth and should be between the second base and first base defenders.

Then, to lessen your frustrations during a game, walk through various situations and discuss how defenders should move to provide coverage for a hit. For example, you may want to go over what the defensive players should do if the ball is hit between the defenders at first and second. The second-base defender moves to the ball with the intention of fielding it. This defender should continue moving to the ball unless the first-base

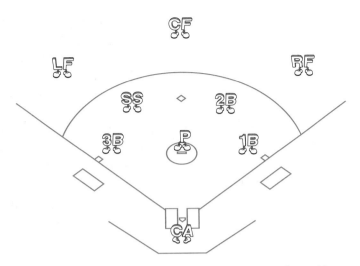

Figure 7.2   The basic setup positions for defensive players before a hit.

defender yells that she has it (meaning that the first-base defender will field the ball). In this case, the second-base defender continues on to first base and covers the base (see figure 7.3). The second-base defender is now ready to receive the throw at first from the fielder (i.e., the first-base player). If the batted ball goes past the first-base defender while she is attempting to field it, the second-base defender will be in position to back up the first-base defender and to field the ball because she was already moving to the ball and she is slightly behind the first-base defender. The first-base defender can then return to first base and get ready to receive the throw.

During any of these situations, the shortstop runs toward the ball as well. However, the shortstop will hit second base before getting to the

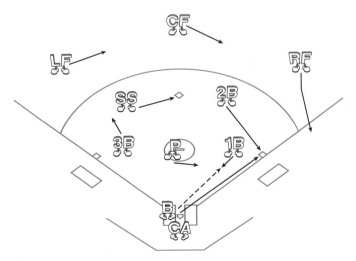

Figure 7.3   On a ball hit to the infield, the magnet principle requires infielders to cover bases as needed, and it requires outfielders to be prepared to back up plays and throws.

ball, so she needs to stop at second and take responsibility for that base. The right fielder starts running in toward the ball and takes the ball if it gets past the two infielders. If one of the infielders gets the ball before it reaches the outfield, then the right fielder will run toward first to provide backup and to cover any overthrows (which are very likely to occur).

If the ball is hit to the outfield, the middle infielder (shortstop or second-base player) who is closest to the ball runs to the outfield and assumes a cutoff position if necessary. The cutoff person is used when the ball is too deep in the outfield for the outfielder to throw it to second base (see figure 7.4 and 7.5). If the ball is hit to the centerfielder, then the shortstop and second-base defender need to communicate about who will be the cutoff and who will cover the base. The outfielder throws the ball to the cutoff player, who then throws the ball to second base. The cutoff player should position herself on a line between the outfielder and second base.

The key thing for outfielders to remember is that they need to get the ball back in to the infield quickly. Youngsters playing outfield positions often grow very fond of the softball once they get possession of it, and they don't seem to want to let it go. Many will freeze in a position that strongly resembles the Statue of Liberty. You can see the expression on their face: "Look, everybody, someone hit a ball out here, and I have it!" Meanwhile, the batter is circling the bases quickly. Don't get discouraged if this happens with your team. Just be glad that the outfielder was able to gather up the ball.

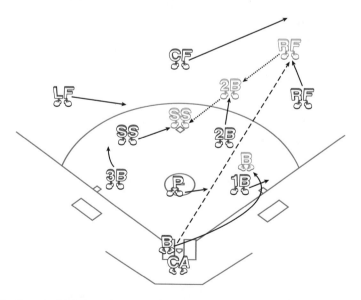

Figure 7.4 On a ball hit deep into right field, the magnet principle requires the second-base defender to become the cutoff, positioning herself in a direct line between the outfielder and second base to receive the throw from the right fielder and then throw it to second base.

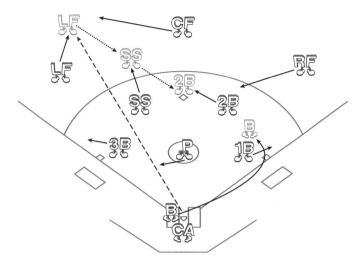

Figure 7.5   On a ball hit deep into left field, the magnet principle requires the shortstop to become the cutoff, positioning herself in a direct line between the outfielder and second base to receive the throw from the left fielder and then throw it to second base.

Backing Up Throws

A common sight in youth softball is the activity that resembles a game of fetch—one player throws the ball, and the other player must go fetch the ball, either because of an overthrow or a missed catch. Even players who are accomplished throwers in practice will often miss their targets during games. This problem doesn't happen only with youth softball players. Watch any professional baseball or softball game, and you will see players make throwing mistakes when the pressure is on.

However, in a youth softball game, overthrows are frequent, and they can lead to more problems for youngsters than they do for the pros. For this reason, your team needs to adopt the principle that every throw must be backed up. Additionally, backing up throws should be a fundamental part of every practice so that it becomes automatic in games. With everything else that needs to be taught, it's easy for coaches to overlook this critical aspect of the game.

Backing up a throw may seem self-explanatory to you, but your youngsters are probably going to need a little help. They'll also need lots of reminders. Simply put, someone needs to be behind the receiver of every throw or batted ball just in case the receiver misses the ball. For a proper backup, the player backing up the throw should be about 10 to 15 feet (3.0 to 4.5 m) behind the receiver and must be ready to respond to an overthrow. Early in the season, you should take time to run through the backup responsibilities with your players. On every play, everyone needs to be moving, either to the ball or to back up a throw.

At the youth level, the right fielder is one of the most important positions on the field because of backup responsibilities. Most infield throws are to first base, and more of these throws will be errant than accurate. But all outfielders are important because they will back up throws to the bases. Therefore, you need to develop youngsters into good outfielders from the first day of practice. Unfortunately, the outfield in youth softball is stigmatized as the place where coaches put their weaker players. Because few balls get hit to the outfield, coaches sometimes use the outfield to hide players who have not developed their skills or who lack the focus to play in the infield. This practice isn't always bad. For her own safety, you do not want a girl playing second base who spends most of her time drawing stick figures in the dirt.

Let your young outfielders know that their number one job is to back up every infield throw. On a throw to first base, the right fielder needs to be in a good position to back up the throw. If the throw is to second base, the center fielder is responsible for the overthrow. On throws to third base, the left fielder has the backup responsibility. As players get older, the opponents will start hitting more balls to the outfield, and good outfielders will be critical. At that point, you will begin to understand the saying "Infielders will hurt you when they make a mistake, but an outfielder's mistake can kill you."

Throws should also be backed up in the infield. For every throw coming from the outfield to the infield, the pitcher is responsible for backing up the throw. For all throws to home, the first-base player is responsible for overthrows (see figure 7.6). The first-base player is assigned to back up

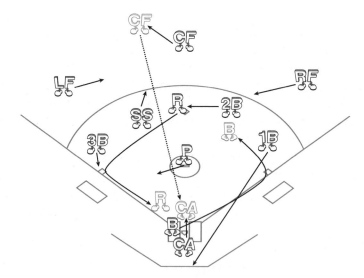

Figure 7.6   On throws to home, the first-base defender is responsible for backing up the catcher.

home because she does not have any other responsibility once a ball has been hit to the outfield and the runner has passed her base. In youth softball, plays at home plate will not happen frequently, but when they do, you will want someone backing up the throw to the catcher.

Rundowns

Rundowns, or pickles, occur when a runner is caught on the basepath between two defenders, one of whom has the ball. A couple principles can help your players handle this situation, but for players who are 10 and under, you should limit the amount of time you spend working on rundowns because the situation won't come up that often. The first principle is that, in general, the defense should throw the ball only once during a rundown. Intended or not, this is usually the outcome because the throw is bad or because the player at the other end does not catch the ball.

The second principle is that the ball should be thrown to the forward base; the defensive player at that base should then run at the base runner, holding the ball in her throwing hand, and force the runner back to the preceding base (see figure 7.7). If the defensive player cannot catch up to the runner, she can throw the ball to the other defensive player, but this practice is tricky with young players. The players at the forward base should throw the ball just in time for the other defender to receive it and tag the runner. If the throw is too soon and the runner is too far from the other defensive player, the base runner can turn around and head back to the forward base.

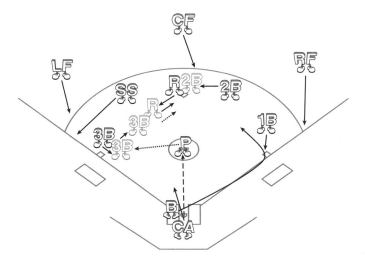

Figure 7.7   On a rundown, the defense needs to get the ball to the forward-base defender so that she can run the base runner back to the previous base.

A Runner in a Pickle

In a rundown, the objective for the base runner is the opposite of that for the defensive players. The base runner should not commit to either base until the defensive player starts running at her. The primary goal is to not get tagged out. If that means returning to the base she just came from, then she should return quickly, keeping herself in the direct line between the two defensive players. This will make the defensive players try to throw around the base runner, increasing the chances of a bad throw or mishandled ball. A secondary goal for the runner is to make it to the next base. Additionally, the runner must stay in the baseline. If the runner runs out in the grass or runs in too far toward the infield to try to get around the defender, the umpire will call her out.

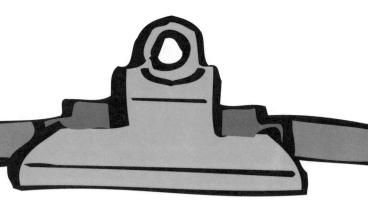

The Coach's Clipboard

✔ The simpler you can make your offensive and defensive strategies, the more successful your players will be.

✔ A simple offensive plan can consist of having a good at-bat and running the bases aggressively.

✔ A good at-bat means the batter sees five or more pitches, swings at her pitch, and makes solid contact with the ball.

✔ A simple defensive plan can consist of mastering the routine play and communicating.

✔ The routine play is usually the throw to first by an infielder, but it can refer to any force-out.

✔ Every throw must be backed up! Outfielders back up the throws of the infielders, and infielders back up the throws coming in from the outfield.

✔ In rundowns, the defense should throw the ball to the fielder at the forward base, and the fielder should move toward the runner to force her back to the preceding base.

Game Time! What's My Role Again?

The day of the first game arrives, and the girls look great in their bright yellow T-shirts. You're feeling ready for the challenge, but then the chaos starts. Your warm-up runs long, and when you send the players to the dugout, the questions start: "Coach, can I be catcher?" "Why do I have to play in the outfield?" "When do I get to bat?"

You win the toss and choose to be the home team. You direct the players to their positions, but three girls are left in the dugout with their bottom lips protruding and their sad eyes staring at you because they weren't chosen to play. Guilt washes over you as you think *What kind of person am I, anyway? What was I thinking when I agreed to coach?* The game begins and before long you see the right fielder squeezing her legs together. You call time and get the girl off the field, only to realize you don't know where the bathrooms are. When the fourth inning rolls around, you suddenly realize that one of the girls has not yet played. And then . . . you wake up . . . and you breathe a sigh of relief when you realize the first game is still a week away.

Although dugouts on game day can sometimes look as if someone let rabid cats loose, most game-day problems can be avoided with proper preparation. This chapter provides advice in key areas such as playing time, equipment preparation, pregame warm-up, and snack time. The information in this chapter will help you out on game day from the time you hit the field until it's time to go home. So, don't worry, Coach, you can sleep soundly.

Planning Playing Time

If your highest priority is to develop young players (and it should be), then you need to make sure that all your players get playing time. Most league games have time limits and usually only go for four or five innings. You need to keep this in mind when creating your lineup. Make sure that you rotate the players frequently and rotate them to as many positions as possible. Players will not start having a preference for just one or two positions until their second or third year of playing the game. If all your players have some experience, you can focus on making sure the players rotate into their predetermined positions. The youngest players usually get bored easily with a position; these players may come back to the dugout saying something to the effect of "I don't like softball anymore." The players who get really bored are often some of the better players on the team, and they want the action of fielding every ball. You may consider playing these girls at pitcher, catcher, or first base to keep them busy.

One of the most difficult things you'll have to do as a coach is to tell a player that she is not starting this game or tell her that she is not going to play the position she wants. No matter how positively you put it, the message gets translated as "I am not good enough." For this reason, you absolutely must communicate to the players early and often about playing time and rotations. If a player has been practicing at shortstop for the last three practices, she will be very disappointed if she is told on game day that she is not starting at shortstop. A good principle to follow is to have each player start at least every other game and to have no one sit for more than two innings in a row. Before the first game, you should let the players know that this is how the rotations will work. During the last practice before a game, you can work on the defensive set with the starters for the next game. These methods will help prevent surprises on game day.

If you do not plan ahead, you may simply overlook the girls sitting on the bench. Then, with 10 minutes left in the game, you may hear a player say, "Coach, am I going to play today?" Imagine how you'll feel when you realize that you forgot to work her into the rotation. Before every game, you should set out the batting order and defensive rotation for each inning (up to six innings). A good way to do this is to complete a game plan form for every game before you arrive at the field. You may want to hang the form on a clipboard in the dugout for all the players to see. This way the players know when they are up to bat, when they are scheduled to go in, and when they will be sitting on the bench.

Figure 8.1 is a game plan form you can use to plan substitutions (and batting order) so that everybody has equal playing time. Figure 8.2

Figure 8.1   Game Plan Form

Batting order	Player	Position played each inning					
		1	2	3	4	5	6
1							
2							
3							
4							
5							
6							
7							
8							
9							
10							
11							
12							

From R. Benson and T. Benson, 2010, *Survival Guide for Coaching Youth Softball* (Champaign, IL: Human Kinetics).

Figure 8.2 Sample Game Plan Form

Batting order	Player	Position played each inning					
		1	2	3	4	5	6
1	Whitney	2	2	6	6	1	1
2	Tressa	6	6	2	2	9	9
3	Emily	1	1			5	5
4	Usha	4	4			6	6
5	Sun-yi	3	3	5	5		
6	Laura	5	5	1	1	7	7
7	Reilly	9	9	9	9	4	4
8	Gabriela	8	8	4	4		
9	Carlie	7	7	7	7	2	2
10	Sam			3	3	3	3
11	Kamren			8	8	8	8
12							

provides an example of how you can implement the plan. You can simply use position abbreviations on the form, or you can assign numbers to represent each position. I like using the numbers so I can count 1 through 9 for each inning. This helps ensure that I don't schedule two third-base fielders and no center fielder for an inning. The number system I use is the standard system for completing a score book: Pitcher is 1, catcher is 2, first-base fielder is 3, second-base fielder is 4, third-base fielder is 5, shortstop is 6, left fielder is 7, center fielder is 8, and right fielder is 9. If you plan to let the players see the form, you must explain your abbreviations or numbering system to them well before the first game so there's no confusion.

At times, you may need to deviate from the predetermined rotation. However, the reasons for doing so should be limited to injuries and inappropriate behaviors. As previously mentioned, you want the players to take chances, and when they do, they are likely to make mistakes. Let the players know that they will not be taken out of a game for a mistake or a fielding error. Tell them that they will only be taken out when they display inappropriate behaviors, such as throwing their helmet, arguing with an umpire's call, or any other negative emotional display.

The rules on substitutions may vary among leagues and sanctioning bodies for softball. Make sure that you read up on all the rules of your league. Most substitution rules deal with the batting order and how many times you can change a batting order during a game. Keeping the lineup rotations throughout the season will help you track the playing time for each player. If you have to deviate from the schedule, make sure you document the changes so you'll know if you need to make any adjustments the following week. If your league has any rules governing playing time, you will also want to document the reason for any changes.

Managing Pregame Details

The preliminaries of the game can sometimes be more stressful than the game itself. At a minimum, you will need 30 minutes for all the pregame details (including player warm-ups), but 60 minutes is better. Whether you require your players to be at the field 30 minutes or 60 minutes before the game, you should be at the field 15 minutes before the players arrive. You want to be there to greet your players as they come to the field. The extra 15 minutes gives you time to determine which dugout you will be in, take care of any last-minute changes to the lineup, walk the field, and set out all your equipment for the pregame warm-ups. Using a pregame routine before every game will keep things moving and make sure that you don't forget anything. The following details need to be managed before all games:

- **Facilities and fields.** Before you let your players on the field, walk around the facility to look for and remove any hazards. If you identify a hazard that you cannot do anything about, such as ruts or holes in the outfield, alert the other coach and the umpire. Be sure to inform any of your players who will be playing in the area of the hazard. You can even take the players out to the holes and ruts and show them the hazard so they can avoid it.

- **Dugout and equipment.** First, you must ensure that the dugout is clear of any hazards. Then you can organize your equipment in the dugout. The bats and helmets should be set up near the opening to the field for easy access. A bucket of balls should also be placed in this area so that players can grab a softball to use for warm-ups between innings. If you have a team cooler, place it near the opening to the dugout from the stands. Place a bucket or bag of Wiffle balls in the middle of the area where your players will be doing the pregame warm-ups. Your team's warm-up area will usually be in the outfield closest to your dugout.

- **Score book.** If you are lucky enough to have a parent volunteer to do the books, this person may be responsible for entering your lineup and the opposing team's lineup into your score book. Otherwise, you will have to do this yourself. Of course, you need a parent helper or an assistant coach to keep score because you will be too busy coaching.

- **Lineup sheets.** Make sure you have a lineup sheet to give to the opposing team so they can enter your lineup into their score book. The umpire will need a lineup sheet as well.

- **Pregame meeting.** This meeting between the head coach of each team and the umpire takes place at home plate just before the start of the game. You will usually give the umpire and the opposing coach your lineup during the pregame meeting. To save time, you may want to exchange lineups with the opposing coach before the meeting.

- **Roll call.** Conduct a roll call before the pregame warm-ups to make sure that everybody is present and ready for the game. During the roll call, you can also go over the starting lineup and rotations. Check to make sure that each player has all her equipment and that all players are dressed appropriately: shirts tucked in, no jewelry, and any other rules that the league may have. Make sure the catcher is dressed and ready to go. Tell the players that if they need to go to the bathroom they should do it at this time. Find out if any players are injured or if there are any other limitations that will keep anyone from playing.

Preparing the Players

To prepare the players for the game, you need to ensure that they warm up their bodies and minds to play. You also need to remind the players to have fun regardless of the outcome. At a minimum, the physical warm-up should include a short run, stretching, throwing, and batting. My teams use a pregame cheer to prepare mentally for the game. The cheer is led by one of the players, and it is usually done after the warm-ups and while the coaches and umpire are having the pregame meeting. A pep talk from the coach is another way to help the players prepare mentally.

No matter what is included in your pregame warm-up, the warm-up should be the same for every game and should be done in the same order. Having a consistent pregame warm-up routine will alleviate questions such as "What should we do now, Coach?" If players arrive late, they will be able to join right in without asking questions. Of course, it is a good idea to have the steps of the warm-up routine printed out and posted on your clipboard for a quick reference.

A pregame routine should resemble a short practice that reinforces all the basic fundamentals of the game. Figure 8.3 provides a sample pregame warm-up routine that takes about 30 to 45 minutes to complete. For younger players, you should keep it simple. The age of the players will determine how many parent helpers you need. Parent helpers can shag balls and serve as the catcher during the warm-up routine. The more parent helpers you have, the faster the warm-up will go.

After a brief warm-up activity, your players can use static or dynamic stretching. Static stretching involves slowly reaching and holding a stretch position and then releasing; dynamic stretching involves controlled movements through the range of motion. Either type of stretching is fine, but make sure that your players stretch each major muscle group: thighs, hamstrings, calves, buttocks, shoulders, and arms. The following dynamic stretches work well. Have the players start at the foul line in the outfield and stretch as they walk toward center field. Then they can turn around and stretch as they walk back.

- **Knee pulls.** Players start out as if they are walking. Instead of walking forward, they lift their knee up and grab it with both hands just below the knee. They pull the knee up and to their body, then release it and step forward. This stretches the buttocks and the hamstrings. The players continue the movement, alternating legs

Figure 8.3   Pregame Warm-Up Routine

Duration in minutes	Segment	Activities
5-10 minutes	Warm-up and stretching	*2 laps around field* with glove *Static stretching* for 2 minutes *Dynamic stretches:* knee pulls, marchers, high knees, butt kickers
3-5 minutes	Batting and bunting progression	*Batting Progression drill* (page 53) in 3 parts: 1. MCP, yes, bang, bang × 1 per player in circle 2. MCP, yes, bang × 1 per player in circle 3. MCP, yes, bunt × 1 per player in circle
5-10 minutes	Live pitching	*Batting Progression drill* with live pitching (see modification on page 53) Note: Pitchers and catchers go first and then move immediately to their warm-up routines.
5-10 minutes	Throwing and fielding progressions	*Wrist Snaps drill* (page 82) × 10 *Figure Eight drill* (page 83) × 10 *Rocking Fire drill* (page 85) × 20 *Three Step drill* (page 85) × 5 to center, left, and right *Relays drill* (page 86) if time allows
5-10 minutes	Infield and outfield work	*Feeds drill* (page 106) *Outfield Feeds drill* (page 114)
15-20 minutes during throwing and fielding and infield and outfield work	Pitchers and catchers warm-up routine	While catchers are getting dressed, pitchers do the Kneeling K drill (see page 134). When catchers are dressed, pitchers feed 10 balls in front of them for blocking. *Kneeling K drill* × 10 for each type of pitch (fast ball and changeups for example) *Arm Circles drill* (see page 136) × 10 for each type of pitch *Walk-Through drill* (see page 140) × 10 for fastballs *One Up, One Down drill* (see page 141) × 10 for each corner: Catchers work on framing the corners. When done, rotate into the line for infield and outfield work.

From R. Benson and T. Benson, 2010, *Survival Guide for Coaching Youth Softball* (Champaign, IL: Human Kinetics).

with each step forward until they reach second base, which is 60 feet (18.3 m) from where they started.

- **Marchers.** Players do not bend their knee for this stretch; rather, they march with a straight leg out in front of them. They try to bring their foot up as high as they can, which should be between waist height and shoulder height. When they kick their leg up, they touch their toe with their opposite hand. So if the player starts out raising her right foot out in front of her, she will rotate her upper body to the right and extend her left hand straight out to touch her right toe. After touching her toe, she puts that foot down, lifts her other foot, rotates her trunk, and touches that toe with the opposite hand. Players continue to march until they reach the foul line. This stretches the lower back, hamstrings, shoulders, and calves.

- **High knees.** Players lift their knees as high as they can out in front of them without using their hands to pull the knee up. This movement will resemble running in place, but the players should be moving forward. The goal is not to run fast, but rather to get as many high knees in as possible before reaching second base. This stretches the calves, hip flexors, and hamstrings. Make sure the players are pumping their arms while doing this stretch.

- **Butt kickers.** Again, the players will look as if they are running in place, but they will be moving forward. Instruct the players to kick their butt with the heel of the foot on every step as they return to the foul line. This stretches the thighs and front hip flexors.

After the warm-up, bring the players into a small circle for a pregame pep talk. Here are some ideas for the kinds of encouragement you can give players to help prepare them for the game. Tell the players that you want them to be better softball players after the game than they were when the game started. Tell them that nothing replaces effort and hustle. Ask them to make a commitment to their teammates that they will hustle on every play and give 100 percent effort. Tell them that they will be winners if they focus on the team's priorities—no matter what the scoreboard says when the game is over.

After the pep talk, your players can say a pregame cheer and a prayer (if this is appropriate for your team). One of the players can lead the cheer. Having the players lead the cheer lets your players know that this is their game. Of course, you will be there to guide them, but this is their time to show what they have learned.

You probably won't need to spend much time teaching cheers to your players. The only important guideline to follow here is that cheers should be positive and directed at encouraging players. The following cheer (called "Pump it up") is an example of a team cheer that is positive and encouraging. The players form a circle. One player is standing in the center of the circle, and the players around her are squatted down. The player in the center yells out a line and squats down, and her teammates stand up and repeat the line. Then the teammates squat down to wait for the next line. The player in the middle stands up to say the second line, and so on, until the cheer is done.

Pump, pump, pump it up!

Pump, pump, pump it up!

Pump that (team name) spirit up!

Pump that (team name) spirit up!

Keep, keep, keep it up!

Keep, keep, keep it up!

Keep that (team name) spirit up!

Keep that (team name) spirit up!

Talk, talk, talk it up!

Talk, talk, talk it up!

Talk that (team name) spirit up!

Talk that (team name) spirit up!

Managing the Game Positively

As the coach, you must set the standard for conduct on the field, and you must control your emotions. Your players will react to the emotions that you display. If a player comes to the dugout after striking out and sees that you are not happy, she will think that she let you down and feel even worse. When coaching beginning players, you need to focus on the things done well. If a player strikes out, you can focus on the fact that she swung hard. Let her know that you like how hard she swings, and assure her that when she does hit the ball it will go far. If a player misses a ground ball, you can focus on how she hustled and went after the ball. Also make sure that you don't start jumping for joy when the player finally fields a ball cleanly. Keep your emotions in check and make sure that your message stays consistent. For example, you could tell the player, "Your effort and hustle really paid off!"

When you are coaching young players, the most important thing is that you don't lose your sense of humor. After all, it is just softball; life does go on. If you catch an outfielder filling her glove with grass during a game, call time and go out and help her. As you help her with her important task, you can talk to her about the situation. Explain to her that her teammates are depending on her to play her position to the best of her ability and that she needs to be ready for the ball at all times. Obviously, if a player is too preoccupied to play the game, you may have to take her out and put someone else in.

In youth softball, the coach's most difficult task is keeping the girls interested in the game. When the skill level is high, softball is a game of fast action. However, at beginner levels, the game can sometimes be as enthralling as watching paint dry. Coaches have to use some creativity and humor to keep the players' attention focused on what is going on in the batter's box. Constantly communicating with your players and keeping them busy between innings will be your best strategy for keeping them engaged.

No matter how many times you tell the players that it's not about winning, they will still be constantly asking you "What's the score?" or "Did we win, Coach?" You need to stick to the philosophy that if the players are having fun, it doesn't matter what the score is or who is winning. You know that your program is successful when the players are having fun while competing to their potential—win or lose.

Athletics is probably one of the best arenas for building individual character. Players learn how to work with others, how to win without gloating, and how to lose without complaining. The top priorities should be for the players to develop their skills, learn teamwork values, and compete at their highest potential. Winning is important and should be a priority when your league starts keeping score, but it should never be the number one priority in youth sports. Don't get me wrong, they have a scoreboard for a reason. But if your players don't develop, if they don't work together as a unit, and if they are not having fun, then what have you (or they) really gained by winning?

Managing Postgame Details

After the game is over, some postgame tasks will need to be completed. The first thing is to make sure your team shows good sporting behavior. One way to do this is to bring your team together in front of your dugout and give out a quick cheer for the opposing team. This could be as simple as calling out the other team's name, prompted by the coach's count of three (e.g., "One, two, three, Tigers!"). Then the teams will line up at home plate and shake each other's hands. After shaking hands, the players need to return to the dugout and clean it out. Another game may be scheduled right after your game, so you will need to move out quickly. This is where having names on water bottles and equipment will help you and the players. Make sure you get the score book from your parent helper and that you have all your equipment. After leaving the dugout, you should find a spot in the grass where you can hold a postgame meeting.

The postgame meeting should last no more than 15 minutes. The cardinal rule for this meeting is no negativity. This rule is easy to follow when your team wins. Staying positive can be more of a challenge after a loss. Even if your team played poorly, the focus of the meeting must be on the positive things that happened during the game. This is not tough to do with the younger girls because they are just learning the skills; you and the players should be able to laugh about the players' mistakes. If a player made an overthrow at first base but the right fielder was backing up the play and stopped the ball, you should focus on the right fielder backing the play up. If the right fielder missed her responsibility, then comment on how fast the right fielder ran to the ball after the overthrow. Or you could comment on the arm strength of the fielder who made the overthrow, telling all the girls that they need to throw with the same vigor.

Never use the postgame meeting to critique the players or to tell them what they could have done better. Any suggestions for improvement can be made at the next practice. A good activity for a postgame meeting is to go around the circle and have each player say something positive about another player on the team. The players are required to identify a specific play or deed performed by some other player during the game. Don't allow a player to describe what she did well herself. The players should focus on what their teammates did well.

When the team discussion is complete, the team mom can pass out the long-coveted postgame snacks. This is a ritual that occurs across the whole softball community, so don't be the first coach who violates the tradition. Don't be surprised if some of your players tell you that the only reason they are playing softball is because of the postgame snacks. The snacks do not have to be anything special—just be sure there is some kind of snack after every game.

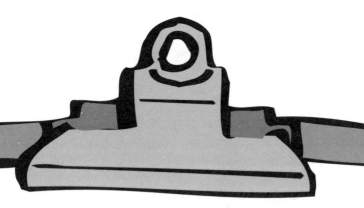

The Coach's Clipboard

✔ Have your lineup and rotations completed before you get to the field.

✔ Remember that your highest priority is to develop young players, so make sure that all your players get playing time.

✔ Delegate duties to parent helpers and assistant coaches to help ensure that things go smoothly on game day.

✔ Use a pregame warm-up routine that incorporates all aspects of the game, including stretching, batting, throwing, and fielding.

✔ Stay positive and composed during the game. You need to lead by example and maintain your sense of humor throughout the game.

✔ Win or lose, your players should always commend the opponent's effort and skill and should shake their hands after the game.

✔ Use the postgame meeting to give positive feedback only.

✔ If you remember only one thing on game day, make sure it is the postgame snacks!

About the Authors

Robert and Tammy Benson have been involved in youth sports for a number of years. They have coached together in the YMCA Coach Pitch Baseball fall league for kids ages 5 to 7. In addition, they continue to work together in coaching their oldest daughter's competitive team, the Washington Angels 96.

Robert Benson began his involvement in youth sports as an umpire for American Legion, Babe Ruth, and college baseball. He then worked as an assistant coach for a 10U girls' recreational softball team. When his daughter was recruited by a 10U competitive team, Benson was asked to be the pitching coach and assistant. The following year he took over as head coach and renamed the team the Washington Angels 96, its current name. During his first year as head coach, the team placed first in five tournaments in the states of Washington and Idaho, took second at Washington State in the ASA 10-and-under division, and third in Class A at Western Nationals in the ASA 10-and-under division. The team's overall record for the first year was 38-19 (.667). In 2008 the Washington Angels entered into the 12U division and were very successful as a first-year 12U A team, taking fourth at Washington State ASA. The team's overall record is an impressive 105 wins, 53 losses, and 2 ties. They have won 12 tournaments and placed in the top 3 in all but 3 of the 25-plus tournaments they have entered. Robert currently serves as the training coordinator for the Tri-Cities Girls Fastpitch Softball Association (TCGFSA).

Tammy Benson has been coaching since 2004. She currently serves as the conditioning and base coach for the Washington Angels 96. Tammy has played sports all her life, including competitive basketball in high school. She now participates in coed slowpitch softball and golf, and she recently participated in a marathon relay.

The Bensons reside in West Richland, Washington, and enjoy giving hitting and pitching lessons, reading, camping, and practicing archery in their spare time.